MACMILLAN SMALL BUSINESS SERIES

Series Editors: Jim Dewhurst and Paul Burns

The books in this series present their subject-matter comprehensively and in a sophisti-cated manner with more conceptual underpinning than has previously been provided.

The series is designed primarily for students taking courses on small business and other undergraduate and post-experience courses at universities and polytechnics. Many books in the series will also be suitable for those working for professional examinations and for well-informed managers of small and growing businesses.

This series was previously titled the WARWICK SMALL BUSINESS SERIES.

PUBLISHED

Small Business in Europe Paul Burns and Jim Dewhurst (eds)
Small Business: Finance and Control Jim Dewhurst and Paul Burns
Small Business: Production/Operations Management Terry Hill
Marketing for the Small Business Derek Waterworth

FORTHCOMING

Small Business Issues: Text and Cases Paul Burns and Jim Dewhurst (eds)
Small Business: Retail Management David Kirby

SMALL BUSINESS

Production/ Operations Management

Terry Hill

MACMILLAN
EDUCATION

First published 1987

Published by
MACMILLAN EDUCATION LTD
Houndmills, Basingstoke, Hampshire RG21 2XS
and London
Companies and representatives
throughout the world

Printed in Hong Kong

British Library Cataloguing in Publication Data
Hill, Terry
Small business: production/operations
management.—(Macmillan small business
series)
1. Production management   2. Small business — Management
I. Title
658.5   TS155
ISBN 0–333–36402–3 (hardcover)
ISBN 0–333–36403–1 (paperback)

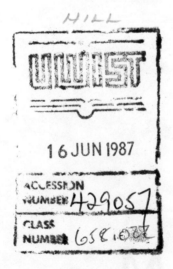

To PM, AJ and JB

Contents

List of Tables

List of Figures

Acknowledgements

The author and publishers wish to thank the following who have kindly given permission for the use of copyright material :

Macmillan, for Figures 3.1, 3.2, 3.4 and 4.2.
Prentice-Hall, for Tables 2.1 and 8.1 and Figures 1.1, 1.2, 1.3, 2.1, 5.1, 8.1, 8.5 and 8.8.
Penguin Books, for Figure 2.2.
Pergamon Press for Figure 6.12.
Department of Trade and Industry for Tables 1.1, 1.2 and 1.5.
The Controller of Her Majesty's Stationery Office for Tables 1.3, 1.4, 4.1 and 9.1.
Harvard Business Review for Figure 10.6,
Management Decision for Figures 10.3, 10.4 and 10.5.
Association of Independent Research and Technology Organisations for entries in the appendix 'Research and Technology Organisations'.

PART I

PRINCIPLES OF THE PRODUCTION/ OPERATIONS MANAGEMENT TASK

Production/Operations Management in a Small Business

Introduction

The first two chapters are the foundation and cornerstone for this book. They provide an overview of the reasons why many small businesses fail to mature, and an introduction to the concepts and principles which are essential if the planning and control tasks, which are at the core of effective management of the production/operations function within a business, are to be fully appreciated.

The intuitive manager

The purpose of this book is to provide a basic guide to the managerial principles which underpin successful production/operations management (POM) within small business ventures. The research and experience which has supported the preparation of the text suggests that the typical owners/managers of small businesses are likely to have developed their approach to management the hard way – that is, through the experience of getting on and doing the job of organising and managing their business. As a consequence, their management style is likely to be more intuitive than analytical, – more concerned with the day-to-day operations than long-term issues, and more opportunist than strategic in its concept.

In many ways this attitude is the real strength of the small business. It represents that essential creative spirit which is critical in getting a venture off the ground and seeing it through its early days – and, equally critical, in **keeping the business going.** This attitude is at the very core of the kind of innovative approach required within a small business: it is this motivation which provides the necessary drive, often pushing the owner/manager to 'burn the midnight oil' in the belief that this is a prerequisite to sustaining success. But that intuitive, creative approach is also a potential **weakness** in managing a small business. The statistical evidence (given in detail later) demonstrates that four out of every five ventures collapse before they have time to mature.

Self-belief is not enough

But self-belief is not enough for long-term success. There is a need to underpin intuitive management with a rigorous **analytical framework** of management principles. That is not to suggest that creative and intuitive management should be inhibited or constrained. In fact, the opposite is the aim of this book – the purpose is to present a set of coherent principles which, if applied **appropriately**, can release the owner/manager's energy more fully into the strategic management of the business. The result of self-belief and enthusiasm alone leads to a highly **reactive** management style, which is event-driven. This in turn often leads to longer working hours and regular interviews with the accountant and the bank manager!

Anyone who has the courage to 'go it alone' these days has got to have more than self-belief and hard work to be successful – and that is not to undervalue the managerial skill and problem-solving competence which is developed through hard experience. The danger with so many people who are committed to achieving something worthwhile through their own business venture, however, is that they are too busy (and too often under pressure) to be able to **learn** conciously from their experience. They rarely have time to take stock of how they manage their business – typically just looking to the monthly bank accounts or annual results to give them guidelines or trends towards success or failure. Busy people can often go through the same cycle of experience many times – facing and solving a recurring problem yet neither consciously noting why the problem arose, nor how it was solved. Solving problems which occur with a monotonous regularity results in at best a short-term approach to managing the business.

Strategy for success

These are somewhat sweeping conclusions which many businessmen may be reluctant to accept. In a sense, there is a strange satisfaction in living through and resolving one problem after another. Looked at more critically, however, this kind of continual, operational 'fire-fighting' must result in a serious waste of the **three key resources** in the business – the owner/manager's vision, skills and energy. Our objective is to demonstrate that there is an alternative to day-to-day firefighting, but that alternative may require a change of style in business life – taking more time to think, analyse and plan. It may also require a change in perspective away from the belief that a small business has little leverage with its customers or in its market place and must, therefore, be flexible enough to react to – rather than to initiate – events and opportunities.

This change in perspective must begin with the owner/managers, and in particular with their **personal aspirations**. The approach adopted towards managing the business will be primarily determined by what they personally want to achieve through the business itself. An aspiration simply to have the satisfaction and freedom of self-employment will generate a different response to the task of management compared with an aspiration which is primarily to 'make a quick fortune'. Similarly, the decision to go for survival rather than for growth will also have trade-offs in the chosen management style. Developing clear personal strategies is a most critical stage in the process of developing successful strategies for a small business venture. In fact, it can be argued that in a small venture the 'business strategy' is primarily an extension of the owner/manager's personal strategy, a contention we will return to in a later chapter.

We can illustrate the power of a clear personal strategy by an example of the growth of a major paint supplier in the UK automotive business. The point of entry to what was (and still is) an extremely competitive market was relatively innocent, but the potential was spotted at an early stage. The entrepreneur concerned was looking for an opportunity to get into 'self-employment' – he noted that garages undertaking car body repairs were rarely able to order their paint until after they had obtained clearance from the insurers and then stripped down the parts requiring repair in order to assess requirements. This resulted in an inevitable delay while they found a stockist, telephoned an order, and then waited for a delivery in their area. The delay meant that expensive equipment and skilled staff were often kept waiting, or other jobs were started creating congestion in small garages when several cars were in process simultaneously: both situations resulted in inefficiencies.

The key to getting into the market was to offer to act as a 'broker' between the garages and stockists by providing a guaranteed 3–4-hour delivery service, but with immediate payment. The service which started with a small number of garages in a limited area was successful and soon expanded requiring more vans (on lease) and an increasing range of services. Today this strategy has provided the foundation for a business which has developed into a major manufacturer and supplier but still offering the same fast service rather than competing on the basis of price. In this example growth was the strategy, but this was underpinned by a determination to survive while others within the same market place were struggling with low profit-margins due to high price discounts, and suffering delays in cash payments by customers. The owner/manager's ability to recognise a need, initiate and develop a business around it and build the operations capability to support the key feature for success was fundamental. This **strategic clarity**, so essential to market entry and growth, had to come from an owner/manager's ability to stand back, evaluate and maintain the essence of his business strategy.

'Births' and 'deaths' statistics

Should the reader demand more convincing proof of the need for small businesses to introduce good management practices then the statistics of 'deaths' of firms in the UK is one sobering way of providing it. For the period 1980–2 an analysis of the total 'births' (new ventures) gives a provisional estimate of 363,100, while in the same period almost as many small businesses (343,300) collapsed – see Table 1.1. Whilst overall there was a net increase of 19,800 new ventures, it is interesting to note that four out of the ten major categories listed in Table 1.1 had many more 'deaths' than 'births', the retail industry suffering the most.

For the longer period of 1974–82, an even more significant analysis of the lifespan of businesses revealed that over 50 per cent of all failures occurred in the first two years of the business's life. Table 1.2 provides the detailed analysis.

Small businesses are clearly, therefore, most vulnerable in their

Table 1.1   Provisional 'births' and 'deaths' by business sector, 1980–2

Sector	Births	Deaths	Surplus (loss)
Agriculture	13,600	14,200	(600)
Production	36,300	31,400	4,800
Construction	53,500	42,100	11,400
Transport	15,900	16,400	(500)
Wholesale	33,900	26,200	7,700
Retail	76,800	92,400	(15,700)
Finance, property and professional services	21,500	17,900	3,600
Catering	35,800	39,100	(3,300)
Motor trades	20,900	19,500	1,400
Other services	54,900	44,100	10,800
TOTAL	363,100	343,300	19,800

Source: Department of Trade and Industry, figures based on the number of VAT registrations in the period.

Table 1.2   Lifespan[a] of businesses deregistered for VAT in the period January 1974–31 January 1982[b]

Lifespan (months)	Total no.	Total (%)	Cumulative (%)
0 – 6	61,061	10.8	10.8
6 – 12	84,359	15.0	25.8
12 – 18	86,421	15.3	41.1
18 – 24	71,526	12.7	53.8
24 – 30	60,080	10.7	64.5
30 – 36	46,770	8.3	72.8
36 – 42	37,968	6.7	79.5
42 – 48	28,250	5.0	84.5
48 – 54	22,979	4.1	88.6
54 – 60	17,037	3.0	91.6
60 – 66	14,043	2.5	94.1
66 – 72	10,658	1.9	96.0
72 – 78	8,348	1.5	97.5
78 – 84	5,590	1.0	98.5
84 – 90	4,032	0.7	99.2
90 – 96	2,523	0.4	99.6
96 – 102	1,391	0.2	99.8
102 – 108	364	0.1	99.9[c]

[a]   Lifespan spread is 0 to less than 6 months, 6 to less than 12 months, etc.
[b]   Figures are for businesses who registered for VAT since January 1974 and deregistered before 31 January 1982.
[c]   Error due to rounding.
Source: Small Firms and Tourism Division, Department of Employment.

Table 1.3   Claims analysis – reasons for business failure

Reason			Small business			Total no.
			New	Existing	All	
Market for product not as envisaged	Fore-casts	Unrealistic	3	—	3	
		Optimistic but possible	2	3	5	12
	Market decline		—	4	4	
Reasonable market, but poor management	Personal problems[a]		2	6	8	
	Poor management[a]		—	5	5	
	Lack of financial control		—	3	3	21
	Poor marketing		1	3	4	
	Business neglected		—	1	1	
	Production problems		3	4	7	
	Competition		3	1	4	
	Deception		1	1	2	15
	Loss of major customer		—	1	1	
	Overtrading		1	—	1	
	TOTAL		16	32	48	48

[a] Personal problems and poor management overlap in that some personnel problems are those of individuals who cannot cope with running a business or have personality or marital problems. This leads to poor management.
Source: Robson Rhodes Report, 1983.

first two to three years – the question is why. A report[1] prepared for the Secretary of State for Industry on the circumstances giving rise to the first 50 claims made on the Department of Trade and Industry for businesses which were financed under the small Business Loan Guarantee Scheme sheds some light on this question. The reasons for failure in 48 of these claims were summarised in the report, the details of which are given in Table 1.3.

The Robson Rhodes report comments that the details in Table 1.3 contain only what in our view was the single most important reason for the failure in each case. In fact, there were usually several, inter-related reasons and it is worth noting that if a table were to be prepared by frequency of occurrence, 'poor management' would rank very high on the list. It goes on to explain that the Report

---

[1] Robson Rhodes Report, 1983.

Table 1.4   Small and medium-sized businesses (Companies Act 1981 criteria)

Business size	Business criteria	Upper limit of statistical conditions		
		Turnover (£m)	Balance sheet total (£m)	Average weekly no. of employees
Medium		5.75	2.8	250
Small		1.40	0.7	50

Source: Companies Act 1981.

addressed itself to four basic business skills when assessing each case – marketing, production, finance and purchasing – and invariably, perhaps inevitably, management was acutely deficient in one or more of these skills.[1]

The significance of size

Having made the point in both qualitative and economic terms that for a business venture to be successful it needs to be underpinned by good management principles, we have to acknowledge that the application of managerial principles and the development of an appropriate style of management is significantly influenced by the size of the business. To define "size" is not easy – the definition will necessarily vary between one industrial sector and another, so that what is recognised as small in (say) the manufacturing sector might well be judged medium-sized or even large in (say) the consulting services sector.

A variety of definitions have been offered from time to time, some of these by government departments attempting to provide a formal basis for comparative analysis of performance. The Companies Act 1981 distinguished between small and medium-sized businesses by defining three sets of criteria – turnover, balance sheet totals and average weekly number of employees. To qualify for one category or the other, two of the three statistical measures outlined in Table 1.4 had to be fulfilled.

A paper produced by the Small Firms Division of the Department of Trade and Industry[2] amplified these definitions, and provided the statistics set out in Table 1.5 for describing 'small firms' in different industries.

---

[1] Robson Rhodes Report (1983, Section 8.5, p. 49).
[2] Background to the UK Government Small Firms Policy, 1983.

Table 1.5　The small firms sector: statistical definitions

Business sector		Upper limit of the statistical definitions of small firms	
		Adopted by the Bolton Committee[a,c]	Revised to allow for inflation[b,c,d]
Manufacturing	no.	200	
Construction	of	25	
Mining/ Quarrying	employees	25	
Retailing		50	315
Wholesale trades	Turnover	200	1260
Motor trade	£000	100	630
Miscellaneous Services		50	315
Road transport		5 vehicles	
Catering		All excluding multiples and brewery-managed public houses	

(a)　Turnover at 1963 prices.
(b)　Turnover at August 1983 prices.
(c)　Turnover definitions have been revised – all other definitions are unaltered.
(d)　The inflation adjusted figures have been estimated by applying the change in the general index of retail prices between the average for 1963 and August 1983, and rounding the result to the nearest £10,000. Note, however, that the retail price index (RPI) is more appropriate for adjusting the turnover of some industries than for others.

Source: Small Firms and Tourism Division, Department of Employment.

All these statistical definitions need some qualification, however; a number of helpful ones were included in the Bolton Report as early as 1971.[1] Its definition of a 'small business' in economic or qualitative terms was as follows:[2]

● In economic terms, a small firm is one that has a relatively **small share of its market**.
● It is managed by its owners or part owners in a **personalised** way, and not through the medium of a formalised management structure.

---

[1]　Bolton Committee Report (1971, Table 1.1).
[2]　Bolton Committee Report (1971, para. 1.4, p. 1).

- It is independent in the sense that it does not form part of a larger enterprise and that the owner-managers should be free from **outside control** in taking their principal decisions.

Throughout the series to which this book belongs, considerable emphasis is placed on the importance of size as a factor in business performance; this book is no exception. The size of the business is a significant factor in determining both the nature of the production/operations function and the appropriate ways of analysing, controlling and managing this critical part of any business.

For the purpose of our discussion, we are 'selecting' a definition of a small business as one which **employs up to 150 people**. The premise for this definition is that the increase in the number of people employed appears to have the most significant impact on the managerial principles which are likely to be most applicable to the business. A small business employing only two or three people but with a turnover of several million pounds will not have the same level of complexity of managerial problems as a business which employs (say) 100 people but has a significantly lower turnover.

Production/operations in the small business

Having isolated size as a critical factor when determining an appropriate managerial style, we can now turn to the main issue of the book: the production/operations management (POM) task within a business.

The POM task is concerned with managing the major part of the business in terms of **expenditure, assets and people**. The very nature of production/operations management, however, brings potential inbuilt dangers. POM plays a major part in the overall functioning of the business but involves doing a large number of relatively short-term, mundane, operational tasks, with the consequent danger that long-term issues may be overlooked or ignored. Production/operations management is, however, problem-orientated. It has been said that 'in this sense its practicality can be overwhelming'.[1]

The manager of a very small organisation, while being involved in all aspects of the business, will undoubtedly spend a lot of time on the day-to-day aspects concerned with the POM task. The chapters in this book define the main production/operations tasks and outline both their characteristics and the underpinning management principles. They attempt to deal realistically with the major problem of short-term perspectives and provide a resumé of the practical approach

---

[1] Lawrence (1983, p. 2).

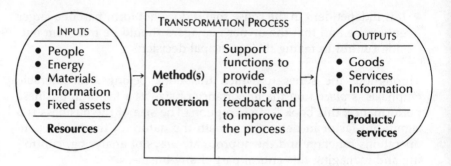

Figure 1.1   *The production/operations function*

Source: Hill (1983, p. 5)

(that can be described as 'best practice') necessary to resolve them. Production/operations is schematically illustrated above in Figure 1.1 as a transformation process, whilst being set out in more detail in Figure 1.3. This conversion process tends to occupy the effort and attention of 80 per cent of all available resources within the business and consequently incurs 80 per cent of the total costs of the business – another contention which will be expanded in a later chapter.

The 'transformation process' in Figure 1.1 represents production management or operations management: these are essentially the same set of tasks. Each is concerned with managing those resources which are required to produce the goods or provide the services. Products or goods are tangible items purchased for the business's use. Services, on the other hand, are less tangible, consumed at the time of being provided with the benefit of that service being retained. Many businesses in fact provide a mixture of both goods and services, however.

For example, a customer buys a new dishwashing machine (product or goods); this also includes, as part of that total purchase package, an after-sales guarantee and maintenance agreement (a service). Similarly, people go out to a restaurant to eat (a service) but this also involves the food and drink consumed (products or goods). In some businesses there is a heavier accent on goods, and in others what you buy is predominantly a service. Figure 1.2 illustrates the mix between the goods and service content provided by a range of purchases.

The mix illustrated here is based on opinion, and others may well consider the appropriate balance to be different. The essential reason for drawing attention to this issue, however, is that organisations **need to be aware of this difference**, and to determine whether they are providing services with facilitating goods, or goods with facilitating services, or a mixture of both.

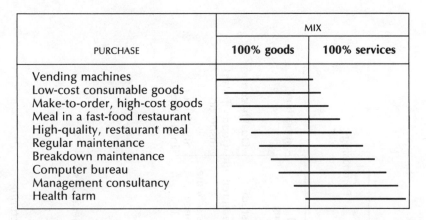

	MIX	
PURCHASE	**100% goods**	**100% services**
Vending machines		
Low-cost consumable goods		
Make-to-order, high-cost goods		
Meal in a fast-food restaurant		
High-quality, restaurant meal		
Regular maintenance		
Breakdown maintenance		
Computer bureau		
Management consultancy		
Health farm		

Figure 1.2   *Diferent product/service mixes provided in a range of purchases*

In a typical manufacturing business the sets of responsibilities listed in Figure 1.3 would normally have to be carried out by one or more people. Whilst Figure 1.3 shows a manufacturing company at the upper end of the 'small business' definition, the sets of responsibilities outlined are similar no matter what the size may be – although in the 'very small' business the functions will be merged, with a consequent blurring of definition. We would also contend that the essence of the major tasks would generally be found even in a business whose 'operations process' is dedicated to producing a 'service' rather than manufactured products.

The production/operations manager's job

Having introduced some general aspects of POM, elements of the operations manager's job now need to be outlined. Although the emphasis to be placed on each part of the job will vary in line with the nature of the business and the size of the company concerned, the important features of the general approach required for the job will, in essence, apply to any business where a 'transformation process' is operating, whether producing goods or services. The **operations job**:

1. Concerns both **short- and long-term business needs**.
2. Requires **man management and analytical skills**.
3. Involves managing **80 per cent of the business resources**.
4. Has a major influence on the **work and money flow**.

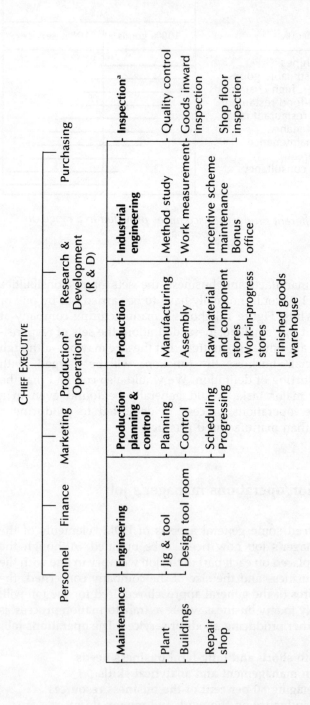

Figure 1.3 Production management functions in a manufacturing business

a The terms 'production/operations' and 'production and operations' will be used synonymously throughout the text

b Quality assurance in this organisation reports to R & D

Source : Adapted from Hill (1983, p. 7)

5. Is the critical link **between operations and the overall business**.
6. Lends itself to **objective performance measurement**.

Each of these statements represents a **key element** of the task. Taken together, the job clearly demands an unusually wide range of skills and knowledge but – and more importantly – the successful management of this function will also have a fundamental effect on **overall business performance**. We will now analyse each in more detail.

Concerns both short- and long-term business needs

Production/operations management (POM) concerns both short- and long-term aspects of the business. Whilst no one can expect daily sales to be exactly one-fifth of a week's forecast or weekly sales to be exactly one-quarter of a month's forecast, it is essential that **daily budgeted output is achieved each day**. This achievement underpins such aspects as costing, capacity and delivery all of which are crucial to the success of a company. The job will, therefore, involve hard work, dealing with questions of detail, long hours and pressure.[1]

A 1978 report[2] noted that the production managers interviewed gave as the major elements of the working day, formal meetings, *ad hoc* meetings (shorter, fewer participants, more or less spontaneous), and tours of the works. The most common formal meetings concerned progress monitoring, supplies/parts and costs. 'They spend little time in their own offices and have little external mail (although they shuffle vast amounts of internal paperwork)'[3]

We have already noted that the demands of these relatively short-term tasks tend to take priority over the longer-term planning which is so essential to managing customers, suppliers, capacity, inventory and cash, all of which are tied up primarily in the execution of the productions/operations task.

Requires man management and analytical skills

Production/operations management (POM) is a demanding managerial task – it requires the development of 'man management competence' and the use of appropriate analytical skills. One significant problem which militates against this happening is that POM does not often attract sufficiently capable managers. Several surveys and

---

[1] British Graduate Association, 1977.
[2] Hutton and Lawrence, 1978.
[3] Hutton and Lawrence, 1978.

research studies[1] list the disadvantages of the POM area – such as problems of declining interest, slow promotion, poor pay and fringe benefits, poor working conditions and social isolation – and the danger is that businesses will appoint people into this key position by default rather than design. However, the success of a company will be very dependent upon the contribution made by the production/ operations function in terms of the effective completion of both the short- and the long-term activities involved. Appointing managers by default in this areas must therefore be avoided at all costs.

Involves managing 80 per cent of the business's resources

The effective **control** of production/operations (which may account for up to 80 per cent of both the resources and expenditure within a manufacturing business) is most important. The operations manager must contribute to the development of the costing and reporting systems within the organisation, otherwise this information – so vital when making key business decisions – will not be readily available. Similarly, the need to control and reduce costs within the POM function is essential to both the short- and long-term viability of the business.

Has a major influence on work and money flow

Not only will production/operations managers be responsible for a large cost centre, but they will also exercise a substantial control over both the work and the money flow in the business. The major work flow occurs through the 'transformation process'. But this, by definition involves expenditure on materials/components and the labour required to transform these into products and services. It is essential, therefore, that the operations manager ensures that the **cash flow** through the business is controlled effectively by meeting delivery schedules (which, in turn, triggers off the invoice and payment procedure). Similarly, it is important to recognise that changes designed to improve the money flow (particularly for the end-of-month rush to meet deliveries) will involve **trade-offs within the operations process**. These may result in inefficiencies (typically increased costs)

---

[1]   These include British Graduate Association, 1977; Hutton and Lawrence, 1978; McQuillan, 1978; Gill and Lockyer, 1979; Lockyer and Jones, 1980; Lockyer *et al.*, 1980.

as a consequence of the changes in the flow of work made to meet those delivery requirements.[1]

Is the critical link between operations and the overall business

The job needs sound managerial ability and a 'drive for results' combined with analytical and business acumen. This is necessary in order that all aspects of the expenditure, asset investment and people are managed, controlled and improved. Too often, the concern of top management is to have someone in charge of the operations function who understands the **technology** of the products/services and processes. This results in recruitment procedures which give undue weight to these features and too little towards managerial and business acumen, so crucial to the successful performance of this job.

This is not to imply that technology can be ignored; but neither should it be overemphasised. The operations manager always needs to contribute to – and often even to make decisions about – process investment. The essential perspectives to be brought to bear are those based upon the incumbent's ability to link the operations function to the needs of the business. The skills involved include those of being able carefully and resolutely to **interrogate both internal and external specialists**. This is to ensure that their proposals meet the specified requirements in terms of technology, production/operations and the business itself in line with current and future plans.

Lends itself to objective performance measurement

The operations function lends itself – because of the tangible nature of its output – to **objective** measures of performance. Given this and the dominant nature of the short-term aspects of the POM task, a business may stress the importance of the wrong things. Any value system which measures and stresses the short term will lead to the job holder giving this undue emphasis, usually to the detriment of the business as a whole.

In summary, the challenge and the stimulation of the POM job follows from the inherent variety and complexity of the task. This is derived not simply from the tasks (which are often straightforward in themselves) but rather from the number of tasks involved, and their interaction in the total 'transformation process'. Keeping a balance

---

[1]   See Hill (1983, pp. 10–11) for a diagrammatic representation and discussion of this problem.

between the important and the less important, the long-term and the short-term, profit (i.e., work flow and efficiency) and cash flow, and the functional and overall business interests is a demanding managerial task made the more difficult by the complexity involved. But, getting it right is often the **key to the success of a business, and its future growth**.

Analysis of the Production/ Operations Process

POM: a definition

The production/operations management (POM) function is concerned primarily with the 'transformation process' schematically illustrated in Figure 1.3. The POM tasks will, therefore, include product or service development and design, establishment and maintenance of resources and capacity to produce and deliver products and services, and the management of the operations process – all tasks necessary actually to produce the goods and services in line with a

19

customer's needs. This chapter deals primarily with the design and definition of the operations process, focusing particularly on the interaction and relationship between:

1. **What** a business decides to make or the services it decides to provide.

2. **How** it chooses to organise the 'operations process' to produce its goods or services.

2. **The** interaction of these decisions on the ability of the business **effectively to compete in its chosen markets**.

The importance of production/operations management

Whether the business is producing goods or services – or a mix of both – there is clearly an operations management task which in most cases is the core of the business management process. In a manufacturing company producing for example, pressed parts, it is likely that the **production/operations tasks** employ **80 per cent of the total resources** – people, plant, and buildings – and therefore accounts for typically **80 per cent of the total costs** incurred within the business. In a service business (say a cafeteria), the production (food preparation) and delivery (food service) tasks similarly account for some 80 per cent of the total people employed and virtually all of the expensive equipment used within the business.

In the newer hi-tech business – computing, electronics – the situation is similar although the exact definition of the tasks may be different. In, for example, a computer software firm the bulk of the people are likely to be programmers using the bulk of the business's equipment – computers. In an electronics firm there will often be an exceptionally heavy investment of people and resources in the product and process development usually working very closely with (or sometimes actually integrated with) the production department, indicating the highly technical nature of the total operations process. In both these hi-tech examples the **operations tasks** are equally likely to **consume 80 per cent of the resources available** and therefore account for **80 per cent of the costs incurred**.

A further example would be a building company where of its (say) 150 employees 120–130 would generally be employed in the operations tasks of the business.

The final example is a 'pattern maker' (producing specialised one-off wooden patterns for engineering companies); there the bulk of the people and resources would be highly skilled craftsmen using mainly hand tools and generally completing a job they start with very little help from colleagues. Again, the 80 per cent rule would apply.

Effects of incremental change in demand

The importance of operational tasks in any business has been stressed primarily because most companies fail to appreciate that it really is the heart of the business, representing most of its investment. In many cases the investment is relatively 'fixed', in the sense that it cannot usually be changed quickly without incurring substantial costs. **People, skills and machines in the engineering factory,** the **equipment and facilities in the cafeteria,** the **plant and equipment in the building contractors** are all assets of a relatively **'fixed'** nature.

The computer software firm which may have chosen the market segment involved in producing programs for home microcomputer use is unlikely therefore to be able quickly to handle orders for large capacity mainframe business programs. The building firm specialising in building motorway bridges is unlikely to be able to divert its available skills, experience, resources and plant to take up a contract to build a large North Sea oil rig. The engineering 'pattern maker' dedicated to producing one-off patterns or prototypes is unlikely to have the capability quickly to produce hundreds of copies of one particular wooden pattern as economically (or as accurately) as a competitor who 'specialises' in bulk production of standard items. The **investment** in people, skills and equipment/plant made by a business is therefore able to serve only **relatively fixed purposes**.

While these examples represent extremes – and may therefore appear obvious – many business **fail to recognise** that over a period of time the demand which they are placing on their operational resources can **change very substantially**. The change is generally **incremental** and tends to go unnoticed. Examples of the effect of this incremental change are widely available, particularly in industries where there has been gradually increasing competition or developing technology or significant changes in customer demands.

The engineering industries have suffered especially in this respect. Once demand was high for relatively standard products and the operations process was designed to meet these demands competitively. Now lower volumes, increased variety and the practice of chasing orders simply to fill spare capacity has resulted in many firms moving, over a period of time, to an operations process which is trying to absorb all kinds of demands for which it was never originally designed. Even investment to keep updating plant will tend at best to be piecemeal and not fundamentally change the capability of the operations process.

The choice of process

All these arguments have been formulated to establish a relatively simple principle – the way a business chooses to **produce** its goods or services has a critical effect on the **strategies** it can subsequently adopt and the **markets** in which it can subsequently compete effectively. The essential issue is that the choice of process inevitably creates a whole range of potential **limitations and trade-offs** affecting products/ services, investment, costs, organisation, controls, and business and market options. It is the nature of these trade-offs which needs to be clearly appreciated if a small business is to grow and develop profitably.

In practice, good operations managers tend intuitively to appreciate what their plant can (and cannot) do profitably and competitively. This intuitive understanding generally develops through experience – usually costly experience! They take on a job which they feel they can do, but then realise that it is somewhat different to most of the orders previously taken on – they find that it takes up more resources than expected, that there are unforeseen technical difficulties, and that it has priorities through the whole production process affecting other products/services. The result: a failure to meet the profit margin on that job, additional inefficiencies elsewhere and an undue allocation of management time and effort throughout.

The first step to **moving beyond this intuitive level** is to recognise that operations processes can often be classified into one of five types:

- Project.
- Jobbing.
- Batch.
- Line.
- Continuous process.

Not all of these are completely applicable to every type of product or service. However, understanding the essence or major characteristics of each of these five ways of organising production/operations is a powerful, initial perspective if we wish to analyse a specific plant or service unit and assess its strengths and limitations in both economic and competitive terms.

We shall now consider each type in more detail.

Project

Organisations which are in the business of producing or providing one-off, large-scale products or services will normally choose the project process as being the most suitable. Product examples include building contracts; service examples include strategy-based consultancy assignments. The **product or service is unique; it is large and made to meet the customer's own requirements**. Normally, the necessary resource inputs are taken to the point where the product is to be produced or the service provided. The reason for this is simply that it is not practical to move the product once it has been built or to establish the service anywhere but where it is to be implemented and used.

The product has thus to be built on site and the service built around (and oriented towards) the needs of the client's business. The operations task involves not only the effective **allocation of resources** to the site and then their redistribution to other jobs but also the **coordination** of the very large number of interrelated activities and resources involved in a way which is both **efficient** and which also meets the **delivery requirements** of the customer.

Jobbing, unit or one-off

Organisations which choose jobbing, unit or one-off processes as being appropriate will once again be providing products or services of an individual nature and made to a customer's specification. The difference as compared with the process choice of project is that in this case the resources remain **on the same site**, and the products/services **flow through them**. On completion, the products or services (now small enough to be moved) are then transported to the customers to meet their agreed delivery requirements.

As it is a one-off provision, this means that the items **will not be repeated** – or, if they are, the repeat order is both uncertain and over such a long time period that the organisation cannot avail itself of the opportunities associated with repetition. Product examples include a customer-specified piece of equipment; a service example is a tailor-made management development program.

Batch

This form of process will be chosen when the volumes of the product or service have increased and sales of these items are repeated. This means that the business can justify investment in **capturing data**, in **deciding how best to complete the tasks** required, and in the **processes** necessary to make the product or provide the service.

The job itself is divided into a series of **appropriate operations**. An order quantity is then put through the process which is necessary to complete the first stage. All the items in the order quantity are then completed. The order quantity then goes on to the next operation, and so on until it is completed. Manufacturing examples include component manufacture or fabrication; on the service side, typical batch processes include computer bureaux which process different clients' work.

Line

With further increases in volume, additional investment beyond that required for batch processes can be justified in order to dedicate a process to completing one or a small range of products or services. The process is arranged in that **sequence of operations** necessary to complete the predetermined range of products or services which the line is designed to accommodate. Each item to be completed then moves from one stage to the next. In product examples, the classic task is a series of assembly operations either to complete sub-assemblies to go into a product or the assembly of the final product itself; the choice of line processes to complete services is relatively infrequent (its use in certain preparatory operations in fast food restaurants provides one example).

Continuous process

The choice of continous process is made where the volumes have increased to such an extent that an inflexible, dedicated process is laid down to handle an agreed **range of products** (e.g., petrochemicals). The process is designed to **run all day and every day** with minimum shutdowns due to the high costs of starting up the process. This type of process is not used in the provision of a service and would not normally be used in a small business due to the sales turnover (£) implications involved to justify the high capital investment which goes hand-in-hand with this process choice.

Process groupings

The five different ways of organising production operations can in practice be reduced to three main groups:

1. Project.
2. Jobbing, batch and line.
3. Continuous process.

As explained above, continuous process will not normally be associated with a small business situation. Consequently, it will not be discussed here, and attention will be given only to the first two groups.

Choice of process

The choice of project as the appropriate way of providing a product/ service is strongly influenced by the **product or service itself**. As a consequence, there is little possibility or rationale for a business to move from the project type to one of the other forms of process. However, this is not so with jobbing, batch and line processes. As shown in Figure 2.1, there is a feasible and rational transition from jobbing to low-volume batch, small-volume to high-volume batch, and high-volume batch to line which is determined by **volume changes in demand**.

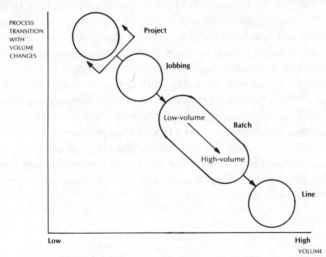

Source : Adapted from Hill (1983, pp. 39–40)

Figure 2.1   Volume increases and process transition

Choice between alternatives is, therefore, available to a business and its significance cannot be overstressed. The importance attached to this decision concerns the fact that each choice has a different set of **implications** for a business, and that a desire to change these is both **costly and time-consuming**. It is consequently essential to take account of the implications associated with each choice as an important element of this critical business decision.

Implications of process choice

Table 2.1 outlines some of the important implications embodied in the choice of process.[1] Aspects of each of these categories are now discussed and the differences associated with each process explained in the context of four specific business dimensions:

1. Products/services.
2. Production/operations.
3. Investment and cost.
4. Organisational infrastructure.

PRODUCTS/SERVICES

A business which adopts the project process choice is offering a wide range of products/services involving low sales volumes and competing predominantly on aspects such as **quality or delivery rather than price**. In essence, the business is selling capability, including a specific ability to cope with product/service developments. Jobbing processes are similarly able to cope with these types of low-volume, non-standard, customer-built products or services.

However, as shown in Table 2.1, the choice of line processess marks a distinct product/service change. The business is now in the market of high-volume, standard product/services, and will be winning orders predominantly on **price**. Batch processes link these two. As illustrated in Figure 2.1 the batch process is used to cope with a very wide range of volumes – the lower-volume end being associated with the product/service characteristics of jobbing and the higher-volume end with line.

---

[1] See Hill (1983, pp. 28–36) for a fuller review of these implications, and also Hill (1985b, pp. 69–81) for a review of some of the strategic trade-offs embodied in process choice.

Table 2.1 Important implications embodied in the choice of process

Aspects		Typical characteristics of process choice			
		Project	Jobbing	Batch	Line
PRODUCTS/ SERVICES	product/service range	Wide	Wide	→	Standard products/ services
	operations volumes	small	small	→	large
	ability of the process to cope with product/service developments	high	high	→	low
	what does the company sell?	capability	capability	→	products
	how are orders predominantly won in the market place?	delivery/ quality	delivery/ quality	→	price
PRODUCTION/ OPERATIONS	nature of the process technology	universal	universal	general purpose	dedicated
	process flexibility	highly flexible	very flexible	→	inflexible
	change in capacity	incremental	incremental	→	stepped change
	set-ups — number	variable	many	→	few
	set-ups — expense	variable	usually expensive	→	expensive
	prior knowledge of the — operations task	variable	known but often not well defined	→	well defined
	prior knowledge of the — materials requirement	known at the tendering stage	some uncertainty	→	known
	dominant utilisation	labour	labour	→	plant
	control of operations	complex	less complex	very complex	simple
INVESTMENT AND COST	capital investment	low	low	→	high
	level of inventory — raw materials/ components	as required	as required	→	planned plus buffer
	level of inventory — work-in-progress	high	high	very high	low
	level of inventory — finished goods	low	low	→	high
	% of total direct costs — material	low/high	low	→	high
	% of total direct costs — labour	high/low	high	→	low
Organis-ational infra-structure	appropriate organisational — control	decentralised	decentralised	→	centralised
	appropriate organisational — style	entrepreneurial	entrepreneurial	→	bureaucratic
	operations infrastructure — dominant operations management skill	technology	technology	→	business/ people
	operations infrastructure — level of labour skill	high	high	→	low

PRODUCTION/OPERATIONS

In project situations, the product/service provided is a one-off. The production/operations process will, therefore, need to be highly flexible in order to cope with the wide product/service range. Because the customer's order is unique the **prior knowledge of the task will vary**, the materials will be known at the tendering stage and the number and expense in set-ups will change from high to low depending upon the nature of the job on hand.

As with project, jobbing processes are also designed to handle one-off orders built or provided to customers' requirements. Hence, the processes need to be of a universal nature, very flexible in their application and able to cope with many (but inexpensive) set-ups. Because the job has not been completed before, the task involved is not well defined and this adds complexity to the **control task**. With a project process the movement of resources to and from the site, the need to deliver many of the materials on agreed days (and even at agreed times on a particular day), and the large geographical area often entailed in this type of work, will add even more complexity to the control task than that involved in jobbing.

However, in a business where the line process is chosen, these dimensions alter. In order to provide low costs in a price-sensitive market, the appropriate processes are designed to provide a specified range of products/services bringing with it the **inherent inflexibility associated with dedication**. Capacity (unlike that in project and jobbing) will be of a fixed nature and permanent changes will require a **stepped increase**. Because of the process dedication involved, the predominant utilisation will be at the other end of the scale – that is, plant as opposed to labour. The few set-ups associated with line together with the well-defined knowledge of the task and materials involved allows the control task to be built on a set of relatively simple concepts; it will be principally concerned with the **flow of materials/ components to the line**.

Batch again links the two ends of the spectrum and, in almost all aspects, provides an increasing or decreasing movement along each dimension. The one clear exception is in the control of operations. Because batch involves high volumes and a relatively wide range of products/services with different orders competing for the same processes, control will be of a very complex nature.

INVESTMENT AND COST

The capital investment involved in a project process will vary between the quite low and the relatively high, depending upon the nature of the task on hand. In most service situations (e.g., management consultancy assignments) the process investment will be minimal, and even in situations such as providing tailormade audiovisual requirements the investment in the hardware will be relatively low. In many product situations the investment requirement will be similarly low whereas in others (e.g., building) it will be higher.

The inventory investment associated with project-based businesses will tend to be a raw material/components inventory scheduled to meet a planned requirement and, as a make-to-order business, the finished goods inventory will be negligible. However, the work-in-progress element will tend to be high due to the fact that all jobs will, on average, **be half-finished**.

One of the important controls in project situations is, therefore, on the **progress of work** and consequently the **level of work-in-progress inventory**. Because the jobs involved are usually of long duration, a system of stage payments[1] is often negotiated before the start of the contract. The relationship between materials and labour within total direct costs will reflect the nature of the task involved, and may well reveal quite different splits from one situation to another.

Jobbing shows very similar investment and cost characteristics to project with the exception that the material content of total direct costs will invariably be low compared to the labour involved[2]. However, the choice of line process brings with it an opposite set of dimensions. On the whole, capital investment will tend to be substantial[3] and involve a high material/low labour mix of direct costs. The inventory requirements with high volume, standard product demand will allow planned material schedules (plus buffer inventory to guard against demand/supply fluctuations) and also the opportunity to make for finished goods inventory, if the business so wishes. One important gain is that the level of work-in-progress inventory will be low and constitute only that which is **on the line itself**.

Again, batch is the process which links the two alternatives and, as shown in Figure 2.1, the characteristics move increasingly from jobbing to line as a business chooses low to high volume batch options. The exception to this rule is in the case of work-in-progress inventory levels. Firstly, there is normally a high volume and a wide range of products/services in the business at any time. Secondly, most businesses attempt to increase process utilisation in batch processes by

---

[1] Stage payments involve the customer paying for work each time an agreed stage has been completed. In this way, suppliers' work-in-progress investment is reduced.

[2] Where in jobbing the material costs are high then either stage payments or fee issue of material by the customer will be agreed as part of the contract or order arrangements.

[3] Capital investment, whilst showing the characteristics given in Table 2.1, may often be quite the opposite. Many businesses have arranged low-capital cost, line processes whilst others need to purchase high-cost, jobbing processes.

making products wait for processes. Thirdly, the policy followed by most organisations is to put the whole of an order quantity through the processes in order to gain the advantages associated with reduced set-up costs.

The result of these factors is that work-in-progress inventory is very high. This, of course, does not have to be the case – a business can decide to reduce the size of order quantities and increase the number of set-ups, reduce process utilisation by having more capacity or devote time and effort to reducing set-up times themselves as an alternative to high work-in-progress inventory levels. As all the possible changes in these dimensions react on each other, a business in choosing between jobbing/low-volume batch, or high-volume batch/line is also choosing between the **different sets of trade-offs** associated with the broad categories discussed here.

ORGANISATIONAL INFRASTRUCTURE

Because of the flexibility associated with the products/services sold in those markets relating to project processes, it is appropriate for the organisation itself to be decentralised and entrepreneurial in both control and style. On the issue of operations infrastructure, labour skill levels need to be high and due to the fact that a company sells **capability** the operations manager will need a technology base to provide these necessary inputs into business decisions.

These characteristics are equally true for a jobbing process. However, once a business moves away from one-off, customerised products/services to supplying repeat items, it will increasingly invest in **specialist support functions** in order to provide the product and process technologies. The operations management requirement will thus move increasingly towards a need to understand the business issues involved in the relevant tasks and responsibilities. The appropriate organisational style will move towards a planned, bureaucratic need and an associated shift towards centralised controls. Labour skills are reduced as a by-product of the capital investment, with an associated increase in support functions to advise on and maintain the processes being used. Batch processes again occupy the middle position with low-volume batch associated more with the characteristics of jobbing, and high-volume batch associated more with line.

Process choice and present/future needs

The choice of process, due to the investment involved, needs to be related not only to the **current requirements of a business but also to**

the future. The implications of Figure 2.1 and Table 2.1 have one important, underlying theme – each process choice involves a set of trade-offs. The characteristics displayed will, by definition, form part of the **process choice**. A business needs therefore to be fully aware of the link between its current/future markets and its processes, the sets of trade-offs embodied within each choice, the degree to which these alter from one choice of process to another and the extent to which a business can alter these characteristics by changing the mix of trade-offs embodied in each.

Unless a business is aware of this, and exercises the discretion involved in this important choice, it will have missed the opportunity to ensure that the way it provides its products/services is in keeping with its market needs and business requirements. Similarly, over time the market a business serves may change incrementally. An example of this change is where a business was originally selling what constituted a high-volume, narrow range of product/services and (due to market changes and a fall-off in sales turnover) has then moved to a position where its current sales predominantly comprise relatively low volumes spread over a wider range. In this situation, many organisations find when reviewing the relationship between markets and processes that there has developed a significant gap between these two prime aspects of the business. If this difference remains untreated then a company will often find that it is increasingly unable to compete effectively in the markets it is attempting to serve[1].

These issues are of fundamental importance to the organisation and management of a small business. Because of this we have included three short case studies. These illustrate the way incremental movements in demand or incremental changes in business strategy affect the operations tasks and business competitiveness. Before moving on to read Chapter 3, we suggest that you attempt to analyse each case using the guidelines in Figure 2.1 and Table 2.1 as the means to structure your analysis.

---

[1] See Hill (1983, pp. 36–7) and Hill (1985, pp. 89–95).

Case Study 1

A plastic moulding company had successfully developed a profitable business producing picnic sets selling through a major supermarket chain. Its products were of a standard type – i.e., limited range of colours and designs but produced with fairly high-quality materials. The products were packaged in a neat plastic case and had become established as a long-running item with their customers, with the consequent security of a two-year order book. The profit margin on each set was relatively small but the volume base of the business had enabled production to be organised efficiently generating a 10 per cent net profit on annual sales of £1 million.

The production/operations task was very straightforward; quality management was also well established – in fact, the degree of product standardisation and operational control achieved had allowed the inventory levels to be kept to a minimum. In a time when other competitors were struggling, there was a positive cash flow in the business.

The managing director felt, however, that the business could do better and that which he considered was spare capacity could also be utilised profitably. He discussed this issue with the marketing director who then came up with proposals to introduce a new range of plastic sets which were described as 'up market' – these offered a completely new design involving thinner sections of material to produce a more delicate item and also offering a range of eight colours. He was able, in his proposal, to justify a higher price which resulted in estimates which indicated a 30 per cent net margin based on the operational costs of the standard line. Orders had been secured from a number of independent stores indicating an enthusiastic market place.

In a meeting to consider the new proposals the production director stated that 'the projected profit figures were grossly optimistic, the costings were inaccurate, and the proposals would undermine the operations of the existing business'.

Under pressure to justify what was considered to be his very negative attitude, the production director began to argue that the company must consider a number of production issues:

1. The most critical problem would be the **time taken and the material costs involved in changing colours**. He pointed out that the pastel shades which were being proposed in themselves presented much greater quality control problems. He felt the up market sales outlets proposed were unlikely to accept even the slightest blemish in either finish or colouring. However, the main problem in his

view was the change from one colour to another. This would be costly in terms of **material loss** and expensive in terms of **machine downtime.**

2. These points (i.e., colour changes and quality control) would lead to a substantial increase in costs and set-up times, and consequently reduce the **forecast profit margin** – by how much was unclear.

3. The increase in variety would not only mean more set-ups, but it would totally change the **control problems which would be experienced within the moulding shop**.
   The production manager said that the existing control system – designed on a very simple basis to handle a highly predicatable order book – was not adequate as a means of planning and controlling the level of increased variety which would need to be handled. A **new control system,** therefore, would be required.

4. The impact of the increased variety on both the machine operators and other shop-floor employees would also be significant. The present labour force comprises a mixed ethnic group speaking several different languages but operating successfully. This is mainly because the **whole factory is routinised** with very little instruction required, product change at a minimum and quality standards, product variances and packing instructions well known and understood. The increased variety, changeovers, quality problems, potential changes, planning issues, etc. would substantially increase the general but informal level of communication and **verbal communication** would then become a major issue.

5. The general level of **technical skills** involved in handling new products was also higher than that currently required (and available).

6. The production director also explained that if **delivery schedules** embodied in the new proposals were to be met, the business would need to adopt a different policy on **inventory**. For, without significant increases in finished goods inventory and the consequent cash flow and floor space implications, production would be unable to maintain its current, fast, reliable response to customer-delivery requirements.

The production director's arguments were, however, not accepted by the managing director who completely supported the proposed introduction of a new product range. He argued that there was sufficient spare production capacity and the proposal would provide the business with an opportunity to diversify which he felt he could not afford to dismiss. He tended to be very critical of the production director's attitude, suggesting that it was negative and indicating that he felt that he'd had rather a soft job for a number of years.

Two years later

1. The company had a critical delivery problem on their standard products.
2. There was a major cash flow problem due to the increases in inventory.
3. The quality function, which was almost non-existent two years earlier now comprised six people handling both internal and customer problems.
4. The business had increased its overdraft manyfold.
5. Profit to sales was down by 30 per cent.

Case Study 2

A small printing company had established a very successful business based primarily on the use of traditional offset litho technology and had added to this a limited facility for photocopying. It had recently reorganised its premises to provide a pleasant, shop-front reception area and selfservice photocopying unit. Its main market was with local businesses and it had developed an extremely good reputation to the point where virtually any small printing job required in the area tended to come first to them. This meant that orders were not won entirely on price because the **loyalty** of their customers and the **flexible response** which they were tending to get was essentially an overriding factor.

The owner of the business had recently started to involve his son in primarily the sales and accounting side. He had spent most of his working life in the print shop and knew the business very well. However, he did have some views about future developments which he talked through with his father. He felt that on the basis of their local success there was a much wider market available to them. His proposal involved some extensive advertising of their services covering five towns in a geographical radius of 50 miles. There was machine capacity in the business to increase turnover by some 25 per cent, and, with an evening shift, this could increase by a further 30 per cent. At the current margin levels there was every evidence that profits could be increased substantially with little capital expenditure, although there would be some increase in labour costs.

The risk seemed reasonable and the advertising campaign was launched. At the same time they began checking their prices against competitors in the area and with other firms in the towns to which they were trying to gain penetration. On average they discovered that their prices were about 8 per cent higher. There was, however, a significant number of much more competitive suppliers whose general price ranges were about 12 per cent to 15 per cent below what they were getting locally. When they received the initial responses from the advertising campaign they felt obliged to review costs and quotations. They were also surprised by the wide variety of printing styles and layouts asked for in these orders and realised that some of these would require more layout and set-up time than the orders from local businesses had required.

They nevertheless decided to press on with the venture, believing that they needed to gain experience of the new business and feeling confident that after an initial learning curve they would resolve most of the problems.

Three months later

1. Within three months of working with their new postal customers, the backlog of orders was building up, some of their local customers were being asked to accept late deliveries and the whole atmosphere within the printing shops had become less controlled and more difficult to manage.
2. Both father and son now found themselves working 12 to 14 hours each day.
3. The company also began to experience unexpected pressure on prices from their local customers as the lower prices quoted for postal orders had, in fact, been picked up by one or two local customer. They naturally were asking for the same discounts.
4. At the end of the year they found that after five very profitable (although low growth) years, they were now barely at breakeven – their local, loyal customer base had been seriously eroded and the business was now dependent for nearly 50 per cent of its turnover on its postal trade.

Case Study 3

A small business venture producing high-performance pumps for 'off highway' equipment had established itself as a successful and profitable manufacturer in what was essentially a specialised market. The product specification was very demanding in terms of performance, quality and reliability and these, together with providing an effective back-up service, were in fact the key **order-winning criteria** for the market. **Price and delivery** were important as **entry criteria.** The products ranged from relatively small 3-inch (diameter) pumps to large stand-alone specials, some 12 inches in diameter. The smaller pumps were produced in batches of 100 while the large specials were produced in small batches of five, but generally utilising the same equipment in the production process.

All pumps had a 'camshaft' which was a major component. The size of the camshaft was determined by the pump size. The business developed a high level of production and process 'skills' relating to the operations tasks for producing camshafts. The production process was also (apparently) cost-effective when compared with competitors. So successful was the 'camshaft' business that other companies who used camshafts as a component in their own products began enquiring about design, costs and delivery of camshafts. Over a period of time (some six years) the production of camshafts increased four times. Virtually all the increase was for customers asking for a 'special' to be produced in a variety of volumes. The high – and low – volume camshafts were produced approximately following the same process plan and machine routing.

However, over the same six-year period as camshaft production increased profits slumped, work-in-progress increased by a factor of three, and the trend was towards a major cash flow crisis. On the surface it appeared that all three major products (small pumps, large special pumps and the camshafts) should be profitable.

The problems were discussed in detail at a special management team meeting. The production manager came under very severe pressure during the meeting to come up with ways of reducing costs. He argued that major problems had been created by sales and product design

1. Sales had over the previous two years 'chased orders' to fill gaps in the order book following a general **downturn in the industry**, when volumes for standard pumps had dropped by 10 per cent.
2. The effect had been that new orders, won against 'tough competition', were mainly for non-standard pumps and camshafts where **volumes tended to be smaller.**

3. Product design had carried out a **value analysis programme** with the objective of reducing the costs of 'standard products' by a target figure of 10 per cent.
4. The value analysis changes had been introduced into production at the same time as variety was increasing and volumes generally reducing. **New jigs and fixtures** had to be made to accommodate the newly designed components and assemblies.
5. **Production had been disrupted** through both the value analysis exercise and increase in the number of set-ups to cope with the variety increase and volume drop. The result was that delivery performance had suffered, priorities kept changing in response to customer pressure, and work-in-progress was at an all-time high.

The production manager, therefore, argued that he could not achieve cost savings without a great deal of collaboration with sales and design. Both these functional managers, however, refused to accept any 'blame' for poor production performance and suggested the factory required a new planning system and a great deal more discipline on the shop floor. To what had become an acrimonious and increasingly emotional debate the managing director's response was to appoint a young planning analyst to report on the problem and suggest solutions.

The analyst was a highly qualified production engineer, well respected by the shop floor supervision. They gave him a great deal of co-operation in identifying key problems, bottlenecks and all the major process 'excesses'. The main problem, however, occurred when the analyst came to identifying product costs! Many components used common processes, irrespective of values. Because the management accounting system could not provide the detailed component and process costs, engineers worked to estimated cycle times and applied 'blanket' overhead rates on the major production processes. The analyst discovered that standards and specials were costed using the same 'standard costs'. Further investigation showed four things:

1. The larger (12-inch plus) pumps were generally given **high priority** because (a) they took up so much floor space that production tried to push them through quickly and (b) the major customers tended to press hard for delivery.
2. An average **six weeks in-process production time** was recorded for small, standard pumps as well as large, non-standard pumps. The estimators were, however, working on lead-times of one to two weeks for small pumps.
3. Camshaft production had more than doubled since sub-contracted work had been undertaken. This had required the purchase of

additional grinding machines and necessitated a reorganisation of the pump, machine and assembly shops. This, in turn, had put pressure on the available **assembly floor space.**

4. Labour tended to be shifted to the camshaft production from the general machine shop whenever there was a 'big order' of sub-contract work in the belief that **fast delivery meant more profitable business.**

The engineer reported his findings verbally to the managing director, together with his own conclusions. He said that in his view the major problem was the failure to recognise that within the one factory were **three separate businesses**, each competing in different markets, against different order winning criteria and making different and conflicting demands on the same production processes. His proposal was more fully to investigate the issues based on the concept of separating the three businesses, (small pumps, large pumps and camshafts) by rearranging production on to an **autonomous product basis** and building walls physically to separate the plant and managing them totally independently. This would require a relatively high invest-ment in new plant in order to create the three separate units.

Three months later

1. Three months later detailed proposals were put forward and accepted.
2. The reorganisation was completed in a further 10 weeks.
3. Within six months deliveries were back on schedule, rectification was reduced to acceptable levels and work-in-progress was falling.
4. The level of motivation in each business – separated by no more than a wall – was remarkable with a tremendous pride in achieving tough targets. The business was back in profit by the end of the year.

The POM task in a small business

Now that the typical position of the POM function has been estab-lished and the functions of the operations manager outlined, we can turn our attention to the production/operations task itself. As implied earlier, this is a **complete set of activities and support functions** aimed at producing goods or services in an efficient manner. Figure 2.2 shows a typical set of such activities. It also acts as a guide for the chapters which follow. A glance will clearly illustrate the complex

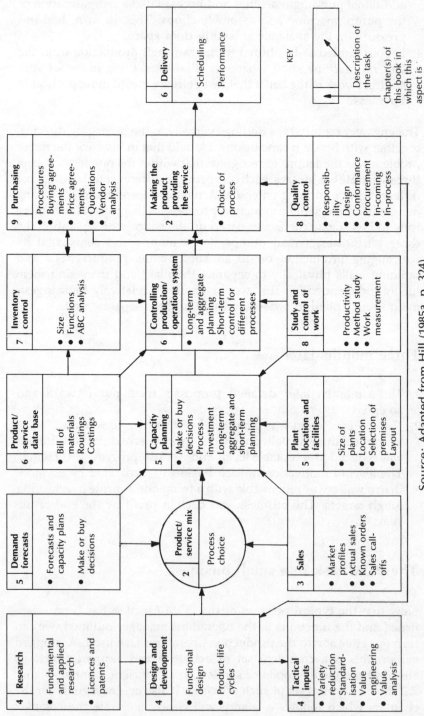

Source: Adapted from Hill (1985a, p. 324).

Figure 2.2 The POM task in a small business

nature of the job and why handling this complexity is a key task within any business. Although at first it may appear daunting, when reviewed a few times and read and reread in conjunction with the rest of the book, it will become much clearer.

It is sufficient at this stage that we expose the size of the task and signal some of the main activities within the POM function. Although for some, the activity areas may be (at best) but names, the chapters which follow will explain what is involved, and indicate the techniques and analyses which will prove most beneficial. To aid the reader further, Figure 2.2 includes those chapter numbers which deal with each aspect; coverage of each topic reflects its relative importance to small businesses, and so varies from very little to quite extensive.

Finally, to help understand the way the functions and tasks flow together, a few lines of explanation based on Figure 2.2 are provided to give an overview of what happens in practice. Whilst in danger of being oversimplistic, this may help to place the various parts into some comprehensive whole, remembering that not all businesses will necessarily be involved in all functions.

Businesses sell products/services; these they either make, provide or buy from someone else. The functions of Research, Design and Development may be at the heart of one business, whilst in another the product/service sold may be in common use or made in response to a customer's specification. Important inputs into the design function are provided by the operational tasks of quality control, variety reduction, standardisation and value analysis. In this way not only will the product/service design be improved but also a clear identification of the **essential characteristic(s)** of a small business will be facilitated.

With products/services identified, **forecasts and actual sales orders** will be the key to throughput volumes and hence to process choice (and, later to capacity planning and the provision of plant facilities and suitable locations). In order to plan and control the provision of the products/services involved, relevant data need to be recorded as one essential input into the effective running of the business. In addition, the **production/operations control system** also needs data from inventory (to advise what is in stock) and work study (to advise how long a job will take). Once on the shop floor or in the operations function, the inflow of purchased items together with the planned production or service provision will take place, and **quality checks** will be performed at appropriate stages. All these are with the one aim of **delivering the customers' goods/services on time.**

As with many other functions in a small business, the task of the operations manager in businesses of up to 50 or so employees is more likely to embrace many of the aspects indicated in Figure 2.2 without the support of all the specialist functions shown. It is important, therefore, that the operations manager is able to review all the facets of the job and then **distinguish between the alternatives available.** In larger companies, this task would involve the effective interface between the specialist inputs and the business needs. This requires that the operations manager be able to embrace the alternative proposals, provide the direction where necessary, and agree the approach adopted; all this in order to ensure that **costly overhead expenditure** is well spent.

The production/operations task needs to be managed effectively. It is essential to ensure that the short-and the long-term are both controlled in order to meet the **total requirements of the business.** In many businesses, however, top management often avoids understanding the essential detail which characterises the POM function. The high investment costs associated with product/operations decisions will often commit the company for years ahead. This makes it difficult – and in many small businesses, impossible – to change. It is essential that the POM role be clearly understood and appreciated by all concerned, in order to ensure that the important **measures of performance clearly relate to the important features of the job.** It is necessary, therefore, to recognise the management and business perspectives entailed in the job and for these to be reflected in the choice, orientation and measurement of what constitutes an appropriate production/operations manager and the task he or she is required to perform effectively to meet the needs of the business.

PART II

MAJOR DETERMINANTS
OF THE POM TASK

CHAPTER 3

Getting to Know Your Market and Your Business

Introduction

The three chapters which comprise Part II outline the initial steps the business must take to appraise its aims, market and environment; this provides an essential business framework for the operations management tasks dealt with in Part III.

The need to plan

In Chapter 1 a main thrust of the argument presented was the need to improve the **general quality of management** within the small business sector. Chapter 2 stressed the need to **analyse and plan the operations processes** in the business.

Clearly, even when the owner/manager is really under great pressure, failure to give time to 'planning' will have adverse consequences on the business as a whole. Although the future cannot be predicted with certainty it is critical that a business be able to adapt and cope with what the future brings. The precise details of the tasks involved in the planning process are set out by Dewhurst and Burns in another book in this series.[1] We do, however, need to provide the foundation for effecting improvements in the business's competitive performance. In summary we are suggesting four steps:

1. Understand what you, the entrepreneur, **wants from life** (and consequently **from your business**).
2. Develop a thorough **appreciation** of the business – its strengths and its weaknesses.
3. Understand the **environment** and **market** within which the business 'lives' – i.e., threats and opportunities within the market.
4. Develop a **business plan**.

Each of these steps is briefly described below, and this is followed by a more detailed description of the planning process as a whole.

What you want from life

This demands broad decisions affecting the owner's values and what he or she views to be the **desired quality of life** – including a recognition of the degree of **risk-taking** with which he or she is comfortable. There are also questions of detail concerning preference for income or capital growth and whether the owner intends (or would be willing) to sell the business as a going concern at a later stage.

Understanding the business

This involves a SWOT (strengths, weaknesses, opportunities and threats) analysis which is designed to match a business's **strengths and weaknesses** to its **environmental opportunities and threats.** Assessing your businesses's strengths (especially) and weaknesses needs very careful and objective consideration. Part of the reason for this is that in many instances, **the owner of the business is the business.** This part of the SWOT analysis is a review of the existing

---

[1] Dewhurst and Burns (1983, Chapter 3).

business and requires a detailed list under each SWOT category.[1]

In completing an analysis of a business's strengths and weaknesses an important perspective to bear in mind is the degree of **marginality of the business.** Donleavy[2] argues that 'a marginal enterprise suggests a marginal industry', which is characterised by:

1. **Competition** between many firms, many firms therefore sharing the market.
2. Vulnerability to economic cycles, together with relatively little ability to **control such cycles.**
3. **Pliopoly** – that is easy entry into, and exit from, the industry.
4. **Scales of production** or provision of service are relatively **small.**

From this research, Donleavy concludes that 'marginal firms survive so long as nothing goes wrong in the market, with the labour force's dedication and health or in the predictability of running costs. Any hiccup affecting the normal management of the business will threaten its viability and more often than not will be cited by the manager at his subsequent bankruptcy as a principal cause of his failure . . . The question remains: "why are so many firms so marginal that an event which a healthier firm would ignore or sustain with impunity is a death blow to the marginal firm?"'[3]

Donleavy continues by observing that marginality 'is often associated with capital failure of both varieties (initial and subsequent) and, in particular, with failure to reach a break-even point. This suggests that the kind of marginality applying here is marginality of scale, whereby the capacity of the fleet of lorries or car workshop demands a minimum level of sales and this level is not met. It is here that the illusion of work often enters, i.e., the belief that business survival is a matter of working 24 hours a day rather than say only 8 hours a day but more effectively'.[4]

It is most important, therefore, that an **objective assesment** is completed as the first step in understanding your business. Survival is never easy, but is made less so if the blindfolds are not removed.

---

[1] For further discussion of SWOT analysis (also known as TOWS analysis), see Heilrich, 1982.
[2] D. Donleavy, 'Causes of Bankruptcy in England', in Gil and Webb (eds) (1980, p. 99).
[3] Donleavy (1980, pp. 97–8).
[4] Donleavy (1980, pp. 99–100). Although his comments relate to his findings in failing road haulage firms and garages, the points he makes need to be assessed carefully by all small businesses.

Understanding the environment

The need to review your business is followed by a need to analyse the environment and record any **threats** or **opportunities** that the business may face, then to see how best to link these to the perceived inherent strengths, and to recognise the level of vulnerability brought about by the exposure of any inherent weaknesses revealed in the earlier analysis. This analysis is critical, but is well covered in other texts to which reference should be made.[1]

Planning for the business

Infant business' mortality (as indicated in Table 1.2) is high: this demonstrates that the risk of failure is high. The first question is why this is so; the second involves the steps that can be taken to reduce the risk and so survive until the business is established. One prerequisite is finding the right **niche in the market.** It is essential that entrepreneurs investigate, in depth, the **real market need** in order to avoid the pitfalls of superficially-(or even subjectively-) contrived demand. Furthermore, it is essential to identify clearly with the business needs. In the early days, in particular, **the entrepreneur is the business.** Unless the actual need and the entrepreneur's motivational pull are in accord, the essence of success will be missing.

Following the need to identify the right niche for a business the next most important step is the **preparation of a business plan.** This will generally be done as a subsequent activity to the SWOT analysis described earlier. Increasingly it is also becoming an essential document in seeking **finance for a business**. In fact, the New Enterprise Programmes (NEPs)[2] based on several leading business schools have the preparation of a business plan at the heart of each course.

However, such a plan is also an essential tool for considering the **future of the business,** not only at the beginning but also as part of a regular review. The planning process and the preparation of the business plan are both discussed by Dewhurst and Burns[3] but have been included here to form part of the overall statement on planning. It cannot be stressed enough that the **discipline embodied in carry-**

---

[1] A suggested format for this analysis is provided in Heilrich, 1982.
[2] New Enterprise Programmes (NEPs) are sponsored by the Manpower Services Commission, and aimed to help people who wish to start a business which has real growth potential. Each programme runs for about 16 weeks with a taught part coupled to a 10–12 week project period. Currently they are held at Durham, London, Manchester, the Scottish and Warwick Business Schools. By the end of 1985, some 70 NEPs will have been of help to over 550 promising new ventures. More recent developments in these programmes has led to part-time structure, but the core role of the business plan within this structure had understandably been retained.
[3] Dewhurst and Burns (1983, pp. 212–16).

ing out a planning procedure has gains in its own right over and above those which accrue from the document produced.

Preparing a business plan

The business plan (see Figure 3.1) takes a long-term view of the business and its environment. Usually the 12-month projection is considerably **detailed** but the five-year horizon comprises statements of **broad intent**. A short description of each step is provided in Dewhurst and Burns (1983, pp. 212–16). Their general methodology is used here as an introduction to the key issues involved in constructing the business plan.

The business plan for a product or service business will generally need to cover the six broad business dimensions set out in Figure 3.1.

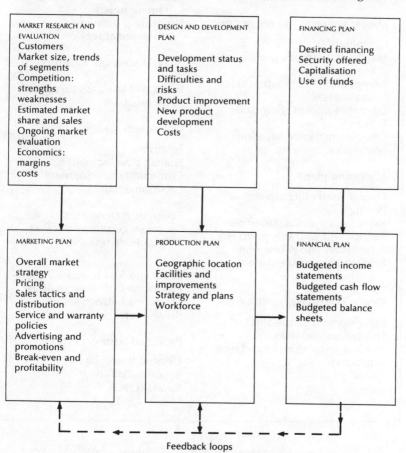

Source : Dewhurst and Burns (1983, p. 213)

Figure 3.1   The business plan

INTRODUCTION

SUMMARY OF BUSINESS PLAN AND STRATEGY

THE COMPANY AND ITS INDUSTRY

The company
Discussion of industry
Strategy

PRODUCTS OR SERVICES

Description
Proprietary position
Potential
Technologies and skills

MARKET RESEARCH AND EVALUATION

Customers
Market size, trends and
   segments
Competition – strengths and
   weaknesses
Estimated market share and
   sales
Ongoing market evaluation
Economics: margins, costs

Marketing plan

Overall marketing strategy
Pricing
Sales tactics and distribution
Service and warranty policies
Advertising and promotion
Profitability and breakeven
   analysis

DESIGN AND DEVELOPMENT PLANS

Development status and tasks
Difficulties and risks
Product improvement and new
   products
Costs

MANUFACTURING AND OPERATIONS PLAN

Geographical location
Facilities and improvements
Strategy and plans
Labour force

MANAGEMENT TEAM

Organisation – roles and
   responsibilities
Key management personnel
Management compensation
   and ownership
Board of directors
Management assistant or
   training needs
Supporting outside
   professional services

OVERALL SCHEDULE (MONTHLY)

IMPORTANT RISKS, ASSUMPTIONS, AND PROBLEMS

COMMUNITY IMPACT

Economic
Human development
Community development
Environmental

FINANCIAL PLAN (MONTHLY FOR FIRST YEAR: QUARTERLY FOR NEXT TWO TO THREE YEARS):

Profit and loss forecast
Pro forma cash flow analysis
Pro forma balance sheet
Break-even charts

PROPOSED COMPANY OFFERING

Desired financing
Securities offering
Capitalisation
Use of funds

Source: Dewhurst and Burns (1983, p. 216)

Figure 3.2   Outline for preparing a business plan

Whereas this format is the one to follow in general, if the plan is to be used to support an application for finance, more background information will be required on the business, its products/services, management and form of desired financing.

Points to watch when preparing this level of detailed plan can be found in Dewhurst and Burns (1983, pp. 215–16).

Assessing the market position of the business

As part of preparing a business plan, an existing firm will need to assess **where it is at the moment** in terms of whether it is in a predominantly growing or stable business. A useful way to review this is to profile your existing (and future) products/services on a matrix as shown in Figure 3.3.

PRODUCTS/SERVICES

		NEW	EXISTING
MARKETS	**NEW**	High potential growth	
	EXISTING		Low potential growth

Figure 3.3   Matrix for profiling products/services against markets

The segment showing the highest potential for growth will be where the **product/service is 'new'** and where the **market is also 'new'**. The segment showing the least potential will be at the opposite end of each spectrum. The segments where either the product/service or the market is 'new' and where the other dimension is within the 'existing' category will be somewhere between these two extremes.

Whether the business is in a **transitory or static phase** will depend upon other factors. Some firms are small because they are at the 'birth' stage in their evolution and are, in that sense, in the transition to either growth or decline. Others may be in the static phase of being small, either because they choose to remain small or because their opportunities are limited. Profiling products/services with markets will help a business to understand its growth potential and enable it, within the bounds of the owner's objectives, to decide what next to do.

Order-winning criteria

The plan for the business will also include **strategy statements** for marketing, products (or services) and for the production/operations function. These strategic dimensions can be placed in the form of an analytical tool for the business manager.[1] Figure 3.4 presents the order-winning criteria in their relationship to the other dimensions.

The business must not only develop a product and marketing strategy but have a clear understanding of the criteria against which it wins orders in the market. The reason for this is that not only is this understanding the basis of the success of a marketing strategy but it also forms the basis of the production/operations task and, thereby, the orientation of an **appropriate functional strategy to support the market place.**

It can be argued that analysis and understanding of the order-winning criteria is the real key to both marketing strategy and manufacturing strategy development. Few businesses appear really fully to appreciate that the operations function does not have infinite capacity and flexibility. Defining the order-winning criteria of different products forms the basis for **defining manufacturing strategy.** For example, if the business competes on price and quality then costs must be minimised by the process engineers but at the same time the whole manufacturing workforce needs to be dedicated to total **quality.** There is a clear and obvious interaction between many of these criteria when they are set out in this way – in many small business, however, such a rigorous, analytical approach is seldom used.

Planning as a way of life

The chapter ends where it began – with the entrepreneur. The business strategy of most small companies is intrinsically tied up with the view of its owner (even with large companies, the business tends to be as good only as the chief executive). A warning shot is fired by Donleavy when he summarises his view of the 'bankruptcy personality' (or, in other words, the characteristics of failure within the entrepreneur). He concludes that the 'potential bankrupt believes in himself . . . sets great store on flair and luck but very little on paperwork of any sort . . . He distrusts professional advisers but often relies on the judgement of friends or family. He is an optimist but indecisive and defers the facing of problems until they can be

---

[1] Hill, 1985.

CORPORATE OBJECTIVES 1	MARKETING STRATEGY 2	HOW DO PRODUCTS WIN ORDERS IN THE MARKET PLACE? 3	PROCESS CHOICE 4	INFRASTRUCTURE 5
			PRODUCTION/OPERATIONS STRATEGY	
• Growth • Profit • Return on investment • Other financial measures	• Product markets and segments • Range • Mix • Volumes • Standardisation v. customisation • Level of innovation • Leader v. follower alternatives	• Price • Quality • Delivery speed reliability • Design leadership	• Choice of alternative processes • Trade-offs embodied in the process choice • Role of inventory in the process configuration	• Function support • Manufacturing systems • Controls and procedures • Work structuring • Organisational structure

Although the steps to be followed are given as stated points in a finite procedure,, the process will in reality involve statement and restatement, for several of these aspects will have an impact on each other
Source : Hill (1985, p. 40)

Figure 3.4 Order-winning criteria in the context of a framework for reflecting the production/operations issues in corporate strategy decisions

delayed no longer . . . He usually knows his products and offers a good service but does not organise himself'.[1]

It is fair to say, in conclusion, that unless the owner recognises and insists (both for himself and others) that planning at all levels is a vital ingredient to both **maintaining and developing a business** then the chances of failure are significantly heightened. In a small enterprise 'planning' may well take place on the basis of regular review discussions, concerning performance, opportunities and threats, etc. with all the key people participating. In this situation the results/ conclusions/objectives still need to be set down in written form providing an agreed and shared understanding of the business. If these discussions are organised around the outlines given in Figures 3.1, 3.2 and 3.4 then they are likely to be both more structured and more effective in planning the business.

---

[1] Donleavy (1980, p. 101).

CHAPTER 4

Developing and Reviewing Products or Services

The product development approach

Chapter 3 set out a step-by-step approach by which owners/managers can develop strategies for their business, recognising that very often business strategies are an extension of **personal objectives.** The intention was also to establish a **sense of direction** for the business, to give the owners/managers a perspective over a reasonable period of time which can serve as a guideline within which the day-to-day operations of the business must fit. Such a strategy can also provide the basis for distinguishing between those tasks which must be given attention because they have a real impact on the future, and those which can take second place because they have little impact. In this chapter we argue that the **continuous development and review** of the business's products/goods or services falls into the category of being 'strategically important'.

The problem is that this development process is often seen as too costly, and even as a luxury. However, the decision on which developments to pursue has to be carefully thought through – there is neither the time nor resources available to indulge in speculation. Yet, standing still or doing nothing, is usually not appropriate. Simply waiting and 'reacting' to market or customer demands generally leaves insufficient time to do any significant development work, and competitors are given the opportunity to increase market share. That has been the essential and underlying failure of UK industry generally, and a fundamental reason why the UK has lost so much ground in what were basic industries to late-starters like Japan and South Korea.

What is needed in a small business is:

1. An appreciation of the **needs** which generate the demand for development.
2. A conceptual appreciation of the **life cycle** through which products and services progress.
3. Some practical **techniques** which can be used within a small business, both to develop products and to review them regularly.

This chapter sets out to deal with these three issues, treating each of them as essential elements of the operation of the business but accepting that the whole area of product innovation, development and review deserves a detailed and comprehensive treatment on its own merits.

The need for product development

The outline of the production/operations process provided as Figure 1.1 defined the **basic outputs from a business** – the most obvious and critical of which is the delivery of the goods or services to meet the requirements or satisfy the demands of consumers. If a business is to trade successfully in any market it must produce the goods or services required. Whilst these are elementary statements, there is nevertheless a fundamental message here which is often neglected by many businesses and contributes to the spectre of 'business deaths' already described. The message is this – that the operations processes of the business are of value only if they are being used to produce **competitive goods and services.** To achieve this over a long period requires specific resources and efforts to be dedicated to the continuous development and review of those goods and services which are critical to the business.

Demand-led development

In certain situations a business experiences tremendous external pressure to develop its 'product'. Clive Sinclair's home computers are an example of how a unique idea created first a demand for the product and then a demand for the product to be developed. His success in breaking into the market was originally based on a highly innovative (initially unique) 'chip' design which enabled him dramatically to cut the price of home computers by nearly 70 percent compared with key brand producers. The effect on competitors was a rush of product development and a gradual closing of the competitive gap. The effect on the consumers, however, was more interesting – as they gained experience of Sinclair's 'basic computer' they began to demand a more sophisticated product. Sinclair had in fact already anticipated both the competitors' and consumers' response because he was essentially an innovator! The fact is, however, that there was no option from a business strategy point of view but to develop the product. To have attempted to rest on that first breakthrough would have undoubtedly led to a rapid decline for the company's products, with new products being provided by competitors.

In the one man we also have an example of the fundamental problems when a person gets it wrong. Sinclair's apparent failure to assess the market demand for his battery-driven C5 was as – if not more – dramatic than his previous success, and undoubtedly even contributed to the later sale of his personal holding in the initial highly-successful enterprise.

Winning orders against competitors

The first part of the Sinclair story tends to be the exciting (and risky) exception. Few businesses find themselves with the combination of a unique product, a manager with sufficient ability, personal ambition and drive, and a ready-made market for the product. The new university-based science parks are attracting an increasing number of potential winners which will do well to digest the lessons of Sinclair's home computers business if they are to move successfully through the 'product innovation, production, increasing demand and consequent business growth' cycle. Generally, however, small business ventures tend to be launched with a relatively narrow product range in a market where there is already some keen competition and consumers therefore have a choice of suppliers – i.e. a marginal market. While it is exceptional to have such a fundamentally unique competitive advantage as Sinclair's original 'chip' it is nevertheless essential to have some very clear **competitive advantage** if the goods and services being offered are to be successful. Consumers will always make a critical judgement about products and services and they will use a variety of yardsticks – including price, delivery, convenience, quality, reliability, technical back-up and so on.[1] The twin dangers are failure to recognise that there are criteria on which products win orders, or assuming that all criteria are equally important, and consequently failing to focus development effort.

Effects of incremental change

A further dimension in the argument that businesses must give continuous attention – and, therefore, resources – to the review and development of their products or services is that order-winning criteria **change incrementally over a period of time.** Whilst the science parks are looking for and fostering innovation and even step change in developments, the ongoing (and more general) problems are to keep track of incremental trends in situations of changing demand. Neither customers or consumers stand still in their own 'developments' – staying close to both is, therefore, essential even for a very small business. The difficulty is that changes tend to happen gradually, and often go unnoticed. Products or services which were once highly competitive and in demand can lose ground incrementally – the pressure of the day-to-day POM task or last year's successful performance often cause a 'blind spot' regarding the need to foster a process of continuous development within the business.

Product life cycle

The strength of the successful small business venture is often its **flexibility to respond quickly to changes in demand.** However, too many businesses fail to develop this responsiveness, even when the needs already outlined are recognised. Part (but by no means the whole) of the problem is a failure to accept that products and services themselves have definite 'life cycles'. The characteristics of these life cycles for virtually any type of product or service are identical. It is the **time span** which changes. We shall now develop in some detail the concept of the product life cycle as a primary basis (a) for recognising when a product requires development effort, (b) for analysing the changing nature of that development effort, and (c) for developing

[1] See Hill, 1985.

SALES (£)

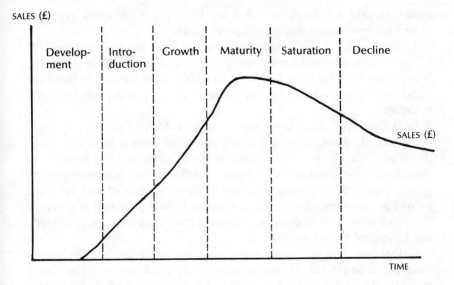

Figure 4.1 *Typical product/service life cycle*

the means of phasing in new products or services while phasing out
'dying' ones.

The concept of product/service life cycles helps to provide a useful
review of the stages associated with the **development, growth and
decline of a product/service.** Figure 4.1 shows the typical stages, and
the rest of this section discusses the implications for a business, and
particularly for the POM tasks involved. We shall look at each stage in
more detail.

1. **Development.** Following the identification of a market segment
for a product/service comes the development stage. The POM task
here is to ensure the involvement of product/service design with
those decisions concerning the **appropriate processes to be used** in
terms of the technology provision and the level of forecast sales
involved.

2. **Introduction.** Initially the typical sales pattern shows a slow
growth. Market awareness is low, and a certain level of customer
ignorance and resistance will be encountered. The POM task will be
to handle **post-launch design modifications** and to meet **uncertain
and fluctuating demand patterns.**

3. **Growth.** This stage heralds a market acceptance of the product/
service and an acceleration in demand as a result of perhaps advertising, increased dependability, and often lower price. The POM task is
both to provide for – in capacity and planning terms – the **growth**

involved, and also to ensure that the low operations costs available with higher volumes do, in fact, materialise.

4. **Maturity.** At this stage, competitors have entered the market, and although total sales are gowing the rate of sales begins to tail off. It is critical here that the **decreases in cost**, which should go hand-in-hand with the cumulative experience[1] being gained are, in fact, achieved.

5. **Saturation.** Here sales are static and derived principally from replacement. New sales are relatively small and a business, will, therefore, introduce modifications to the existing designs in order to stimulate new interest and also to differentiate increasingly its product/service from those supplied by its competitors. An important POM task is to ensure that continued and close attention is given to the product/service in order to maintain low costs and hence achieve the **budgeted profit margin.**

6. **Decline.** The saturation stage may be of differing lengths before sales begin to fall off. Improved alternative products or services will become more attractive, and bring about its eventual decline. The POM task in this phase will be effectively to handle the **lower volumes** involved. This will usually necessitate change in the process choice approach from the one used when volumes were high.

Techniques for product renewal and review

The phases in a product/service life cycle are in practice more subtle (and the boundaries more difficult to define) than is implied by the schematic outline of Figure 4.1. However, failure to recognise the trends in particular product life cycles and the interrelationship of different product life cycles in a business has massive implications for the production/operations processes of an organisation.[2] Failure to recognise the different stages of growth and decline will also result in failure to take out redundant products/services, which in turn, will lead to a business becoming **less profitable.** A lack of new products/ services can have a similarly dramatic effect where the business gets out of line with its market place or customers, or fails to phase in replacements for those products/services in decline.

There are, however, several well-established techniques which can be used at appropriate points in the product cycle:

---

[1] The phenomenon of experience curves is explained in detail in Hill (1985, Chapter 4).

[2] The implications for production/operations processes of change in product/service life cycle are discussed only briefly here. Hill (1985) gives a more in-depth analysis.

1. Innovation.
2. Diversification.
3. Variety reduction.
4. Standardisation.
5. Value analysis.

Each of these techniques provides methodology for achieving specific objectives at different points in the life cycle. It can be argued that they simply represent applied common sense – their value is that they provide a structured, orderly means of managing operationally this aspect of a business. In order for practical people to work effectively they generally need 'tools' and 'guidelines' – the comments which follow are no more than this. However, time spent in consciously and specifically using the methodologies outlined, at appropriate points in the life cycle, will bring its own 'payback'.

INNOVATION

Innovation is not easy to predict.[1] It requires a blend of curiosity and open-mindedness which links sets of phenomena, and results in a technical possibility fulfilling an economic or social need. It can take many forms:

- An existing product manufactured from **new materials or a new combination of existing materials.**
- Adaptation of an existing product to meet either a **new or an existing need.**
- A new product to meet a **required or perceived need**, often based on sound **market research**.
- A new **process technology**, either to provide lower costs or to make a new product.[2]

The success of any business, no matter what its size, depends to a large extent on its ability to introduce new goods or services. The small firm is often severely limited, compared to larger firms, in the extent to which it can devote money and resources to new product research and evaluation. Rarely will it have a research and development (R & D) function whose prime role it would be to act as a chrysalis for new ideas. Similarly, the necessary investment to support these development activities will not be as readily available. In

---

[1] Having said this, however, Robinson (1975) outlines findings that fashion follows a cycle regardless of economic trends and technological innovations, and provides a pointed note to product planners systematically to reduce these aspects of unpredictability wherever possible.

[2] A useful article is Lowe and Crawford, 1982.

addition, product/service ideas which demand a high level of technical know how will often be screened out at an early stage. Clearly, then, the large business tends to have distinct advantages over the small in this area.

Given these perspectives, however, research data reveals that not only do small businesses contribute an important share of innovations but do so apparently more effectively than larger businesses, when compared to the level of R & D expenditure involved. An article[1] on small and medium-sized manufacturing companies and technological innovation confirms the high concentration of R & D expenditure in large companies. In 1970, companies employing more than 5,000 accounted for 89 per cent, 75 per cent and 60 per cent of all industrial R & D expenditure in the USA, West Germany and France respectively. This is what one would expect. However, an OECD paper[2] revealed that, based upon patent statistics, the estimated innovation rates in major innovations per R & D dollar in the period 1953–73 were 57 per cent, 15 per cent and 2 per cent for firms employing 1–1,000, 1,000–10,000 and 10,000 and over respectively (innovations in the 1–1,000 category for the period 1953–59 were used as the base year for this assessment[3]). Other figures also support these findings. The Bolton Committee revealed that whereas the small firms' share of R & D expenditure in the UK was some 5 per cent or less, percentage of innovations was twice that (see Table 4.1).

Table 4.1 *Percentage share of sample innovations, by size of firm*

Period	Size of firm – number of employees						All firms	
	Small 1–199		Medium 200–999		Large 1,000+			
	Innovations							
	No.	Total (%)	No.	Total (%)	No.	Total (%)	No.	Total (%)
1945–53	17	9	25	12	160	79	202	100
54–61	38	10	43	11	313	80	394	100
61–70	54	11	53	10	399	79	506	100
TOTAL	109	10	121	11	872	79	1,102	100

Source: Bolton Committee Report (1971, VIII, Table 4, p. 53)

[1] Rothwell (1978, pp. 349–59).
[2] OECD, 1978.
[3] Although counting patents does not necessarily represent the level of quality of the innovation being achieved, the figures provided do show a distinctly high rate of innovations per R & D dollar for small and medium sized firms.

A report in 1976 revealed that small firms (defined as having sales less that $5 million) contributed an average of 31 per cent of innovations in the period 1953–73 in five major countries: France, Japan, UK, USA and West Germany.[1]

Innovation has two main sources. It is either empirical or it is drawn from applied research. Both are concerned with the solution to practical problems, with applied research classifying and interpreting basic knowledge from fundamental research activities to facilitate problem-solving. However, the question of the way in which ideas are transferred from a predominantly research environment to a commercial one was raised by Gibbons and Watkins.[2] They cite the research study on technological innovation by Langrish, Gibbons, Evans and Jevons[3] which revealed that of 158 important technical ideas contributing to the innovations which won Queen's Awards for Technological Innovation, 102 were from outside the firm. There were a variety of methods for 'transferring' the innovation to the firm – new people joining the firm, extrapolating from wider experience in the industry, commercial agreements, collaboration with suppliers or customers were some of the key means. These are set out in more detail in Figure 4.2.

In the UK there are a number of institutions which exist to provide help and useful services to inventors; a list of these are given in Appendix 1 (p. 70). There are also many research associations which are the centre of knowledge for their respective fields. They have good information systems and will be able to provide help or offer advice on where to go as a next step (see Appendix 2, p. 73).

DIVERSIFICATION

The need for a small business to diversify its current products or services may arise for several reasons. One may be concerned with the more effective use of **existing operations capacity**, or to reflect the **current sales pattern** (e.g., seasonability of or decline in demand). Another may be concerned with **building on existing markets or advantages**. These include responding to customers' requests, widening current product/service range to increase sales in total, or to increase turnover (£) in line with planned internal expansion and the corresponding increase in overheads. The final category concerns the move into new product/service areas derived from research, innovation of all kinds, the planned use of by-products/services from existing

---

[1] National Science Foundation, 1976. An earlier paper by Cooper (1964) supports this general theme.
[2] Gibbons and Watkins (1970, pp. 340–8).
[3] Langrish *et al.*, 1972.

METHOD OF TRANSFER	NO. OF TECHNICAL IDEAS
Transfer by person **joining the firm**	20.5
Common knowledge via – industrial experience	15.0
– education	9.0
Commercial agreement (including takeover and sale of know how)	10.5
Literature (technical, scientific and patent)	9.5
Personal contact in UK	8.5
Collaboration with – supplier	7.0
– customer	5.0
Visit overseas	6.5
Passed on by **government organisation**	6.0
Conference in UK	2.5
Consultancy	2.0
TOTAL	102.0

Half integers arise where the method of transfer involved more than one route.

Source: Based on Langrish *et al.* (1972, p. 63)

Figure 4.2   Transferring technical ideas to a business

processes and a decision to capitalise on the internal resources of the company.[1]

When considering diversification, it is important for a small business to **identify the market for each product by customer order size** and ensure that it selects only those compatible with its **own internal resources and capacities**. In this way, it will avoid falling into the expensive and often disastrous trap of taking on an order which, though attractive in itself due to the high invoice value involved, is in fact not in line with the capacity requirements necessary effectively to handle the associated volumes, nor in keeping with the experience or capabilities of the operations function. **Not all sales are equally good,**

---

[1] Note, however, the dangers of introducing products/services primarily because they are offered by your competitors. Known as 'me-too' products, they will often fail to survive, as Davison (1976) clearly argues; his article concludes that 'unless your brand is cheaper or better, it's probably not going to survive'.

and a business needs always to remember that the most significant sales decision may be those orders to **which it says no**! (As, these define a business's market boundaries.)

Successful diversification will often be linked to the underlying **culture of the management** involved. On a conservative–progressive spectrum, old-established, family-owned businesses will often be well over towards the conservative end by contrast with more modern, recently-established companies. It is therefore important to recognise where a business is on this continuum, and the mix of advantages and disadvantages which are involved. The choice of how to diversify should be made with this clearly in mind. To change the future pattern of innovation will require the development of a different mix of in-house strengths and weaknesses.[1]

VARIETY REDUCTION

One way of reconciling falling sales demand with what is best for the business is to use the technique of variety reduction. This is a review of existing products/services based on the recognition that some will generate more sales than others. The procedure is to draw up a **Pareto list**[2] by putting all the products/services into rank order based upon sales turnover (as shown in Figure 4.3). This reveals that the top six (or 33 per cent) of the products account for almost 80 per cent of the total turnover. Also known as the 80/20 rule,[3] it is a simple but effective way of drawing management's attention to the areas where highest control is needed,[4] or (as in this example) as to whether or not an item should stay in the current product/service range, a question which the technique of variety reduction helps to answer. From the list given in Figure 4.3 it can be seen that the top five products accounts for 71 per cent of total sales, while the last eight account for only 4 per cent. Variety reduction would propose that this long 'Pareto tail' should be reviewed with a view to being phased out.

The procedure is to check the relative performance over the last few years of the 'low percentage of total sales' items, in order to deter-

---

[1] Dewhurst and Burns (1983, pp. 60–2) also discusses diversification and growth strategies for the small business.
[2] A Pareto list involves placing the items in question into decreasing order of value (in Figure 4.3 it is sales turnover) which will often reveal the 'significant few' and 'trivial many' phenomenon which characterises many business situations.
[3] The 80/20 relationship implied in this rule is only an indication of the size of the actual figures involved. Thus, in the example in Figure 4.3, 33 per cent of the products generated some 80 per cent of the sales.
[4] The 80/20 rule is also used to great effect in the control of inventory (see Chapter 7).

PRODUCT REFERENCE	ANNUAL SALES TURNOVER	PERCENTAGE OF TOTAL SALES	
		ACTUAL (%)	CUMULATIVE (%)
AB160	145,000	22.1	22.1
CD175	89,00	13.6	35.7
CD150	87,000	13.3	49.0
EF295	75,000	11.5	60.5
AB090	68,000	10.4	70.9
AB140	51,000	7.8	78.7
CD250	40,000	6.1	84.8
EF310	29,000	4.4	89.2
EF328	17,000	2.6	91.8
CD200	15,000	2.3	94.1
CD225	13,000	2.0	96.1
EF250	7,500	1.2	97.3
AB125	5,000	0.7	98.0
AB130	3,500	0.5	98.5
CD275	3,500	0.5	99.0
CD300	3,000	0.4	99.4
EF350	2,500	0.4	99.8
EF400	1,000	0.2	100.0
TOTAL	655,000	100.0	100.0

Figure 4.3   Product analysis by annual sales turnover

mine if the individual trend is upward, level, or downward. Further checks are then made on those items falling into the 'level' or 'down-ward' categories to see if their contribution[1] can be improved. If this does not bring about the desired level of contribution to selling price (bearing in mind the degree of technical, inventory and other invest-ment required to support each product/service, plus the high level of operations inconvenience involved in providing them) then they should be candidates for phasing out of the sales range. The sales argument for retaining items in the range will often be strong, but neither this nor the operations point of view should necessarily dominate. It is variety reduction's **net effect on the business** which needs to be considered, and on which the decision should be based.

STANDARDISATION

Standardised materials, components and sub-assemblies can be used to make finished items which are different in appearance and per-formance. The approach is often best achieved by stipulating that a careful review is made at the design stage to ensure that each part is

[1] Contribution = selling price *less* variable costs.

checked in terms of whether there is a current material, component or sub-assembly which could do the same job, or whether there is a standard item from an outside supplier to provide the function required. Due to the output volumes involved over the years for every item, it is essential that this procedure is followed in order to capture the **cumulative volumes associated with each item's life cycle**. One way of helping to ensure that this is adopted is by formalising the checking procedure and requiring that against each part or service involved the nearest existing (internal and external) item available is detailed. This is in order to demonstrate that the check has been made, and to form the basis for discussion and questions.

VALUE ANALYSIS

The Census of Production[1] revealed that in 1981 the purchases made by all UK manufacturing industries were 4.2 times higher than the cost of operatives and 3.7 times higher than all wages and salaries. However, despite this, most businesses still place little attention (and devote relatively few resources) to reducing the material content of their cost bill.

An important technique to help provide a systematic approach to reducing the costs of both products and services (but without impairing their function) is value analysis (VA).[2] This is defined in BS 3138[3] as 'a systematic, interdisciplinary examination of factors affecting the cost of a product or service, in order to devise means of achieving the specified purpose most economically at the required standard of quality and reliability'.

In determining which aspects of production/operations management were most relevant to participants on 12 different New Enterprise Programmes (NEPs),[4] the 16 or so members on each course were given an initial list of seven areas from which to choose the three or four to be covered by the available teaching sessions. In eleven instances, value analysis was chosen as one to be covered and in the remaining course, an additional session devoted to value analysis

---

[1] *Business Monitor Report*, 1981.

[2] 'Value engineering' is often used synonymously with value analysis but, strictly speaking, it refers to the application of this technique in the *design* stage of a product/service.

[3] *Glossary of Terms used in Work Study and Organisation and Methods*, 1979.

[4] New Enterprise Programmes (NEPs), sponsored by the Manpower Services Commission are described in detail on p. 48, footnote 2.

was used to meet the needs of those participants who wished to understand more about this technique but whose interests had been outvoted by the others in the group.

The value analysis (VA) procedure to be followed is in two parts:

- The **structure** of a value analysis **group**.
- The **steps** in a value analysis **procedure**.

1. STRUCTURE OF A VALUE ANALYSIS GROUP

Value analysis (VA) is best undertaken by a small group working together on a product or service. The preferred structure of a VA group or team is a **mix of skills**, probably including a specialist in VA plus members from design, purchasing, costing and operations. The group will always require good leadership, and it must also be prepared to adopt a range of working styles to suit the particular stage of the VA procedure. At times a non-evaluative style will be essential (to generate ideas), at other times a highly analytical style will be necessary. Members will not only have different technical knowledge but will also have different personal skills which need to be drawn on as the different stages of the VA procedure are worked through.

2. STEPS INVOLVED IN A VALUE ANALYSIS PROCEDURE

Eight steps are involved in the value analysis (VA) procedure:

1. **Select the item**. Items are selected in line with the principle of unit cost and volumes. The application of the 80/20 rule will again help here. This principle reflects the fact that 20 per cent of the products/services will account for 80 per cent of the sales turnover and reinforces the importance of choosing the more critical items for attention.

Value analysis should not be used as a technique to prop up ailing products/services which are nearing the end of their life cycles. Instead, it should address the problem of reducing costs of those products/services which are **profitable and with level or growing sales anticipated in the future**.

2. **Gathering information**. It is important throughout this procedure to ensure that in no way should its application bring with it any air of recrimination. Information should include both costs and a statement of the exact function served by each part. For ease of subsequent analysis, such items should be set out in a **spread sheet**, **matrix form**, giving a list of parts, functional descriptions and relevant costs.

3. **Analyse its function and value for money**. At this stage, each part and its relationship to the whole product/service is reviewed in order that everyone in the team can understand the function it performs, why it is included in the design, and the costs involved. The analysis of each 'function' on a 'value-for-money' basis can be undertaken in a variety of ways – the VA team should normally determine their **own rules** as this will generate an enriched appreciation and understanding of the process through which they are working. Once the 'rules' are agreed, however, they must be **applied consistently**.

4. **Generate alternative ways to provide the same function through brainstorming.**[1] In order to ensure that the ideas for improvement are not inhibited, the correct procedure involved in brainstorming should be closely followed. It is most important here to remember that the ideas are evaluated at the next stage and not at the point of their generation. It is also necessary to contact the supplier(s) involved in order to discuss the **constraints inherent in the current design** and the **cost consequences** which ensue. Information concerning the relationship between design and a supplier's processes will often reveal the features of the bought-out item which are responsible for the higher proportions of the costs involved and the degree of match between the product design and process capability.

5. **Assess the ideas**. The ideas need then to be assessed, firstly in terms of whether they are practical, and then in terms of their function and value. Often, as in the brainstorming, ideas-generation session, one suggestion will lead to another. Ideas might be 'ranked' to differentiate between **fundamentally important ideas** (which should have prime attention) and those ideas which though good in themselves may have only a **marginal impact in the VA exercise**.

6. **Decide on what action to take**. Part of the last step includes separating the probables and possibles from the non-runners. It is important now to keep the momentum going and the decision 'what to do next' is critical in this respect. Proposals should be set out in a formal way to ensure that all issues are fully explored and quantified if possible. It is also essential to test and try out new proposals taking into full account **field, market or customer performance criteria**. Because the VA team is a temporary group, there is sometimes the danger of generating an apparently good idea without the necessary sense of **accountability to test it rigorously**.

7. **Implement the decision**. It is important that the next step of implementing the decision is made in an orderly manner, and that the phasing in ensures that the inventory holdings of obsolescent

---

[1] 'Brainstorming' is a formal procedure for generating many ideas from which a few useful ones can be culled and used in the VA procedure.

parts due to the change are kept to a minimum. In addition, customers need to be clearly advised and given ample warning before-
hand, particularly where the change is an important one. Provision of
future service and replacement parts needs to be recognised and
accounted for in the system.

8. **Evaluate the results**. The final step is to evaluate the results. This
is not only to ensure that the rewards for the work involved are
actually gained and not allowed to slip away, but also to provide a
stimulus for future work of this kind. Once this pattern of activity has
been established significant inroads will be made to the cost of both
existing and future products/services. It will also help reinforce the
need for **continued review of design** in order to improve the chances
of capturing the substantial gains involved.

Conclusion

Perhaps two of the most crucial misnomers in the English language
are 'simplicity' and 'common sense'. Certainly any third-rate designer
can create complexity and all the associated costs that go with it.
Fultilling the functional requirements of a product/service is only the
first step in the design procedure. As important in this total approach
is the task of pursuing all ways of simplifying the initial ideas in order
to reduce costs whilst still meeting the functional requirements of the
design in question.

In many small businesses, there is often an aura surrounding
design and creativity which can, if not checked, result in what is
tantamount to mystique. The result will often mean that designs go
unchallenged. It is important, however, that **all functions of the
business** are evaluated and their ideas, procedures, philosophies and
contributions questioned **for the benefit of the business as a whole**.
The area of design is no exception to this. Costly ways of providing
products/services will not only reduce the profits of a small business,
but will also make it less competitive in its future markets.

Appendix 1: Institutions which provide help and useful services to inventors

Several well-established institutions exist to provide help and advice to
inventors. These services include more formal help in the areas of finance
and technology support and advice on developing, patenting and marketing
your product together with less formal help such as the opportunity to

discuss common problems and guidance on the pitfalls to be avoided. Brief details on these organisations is provided below.[1]

BRITISH TECHNOLOGY GROUP, 101 Newington Causeway, London SE1 6BU (01–403–6666). Contact: A. Chrismas. BTG's objective is to promote the development of new technology into commercial products, particularly where the technology originates from public-sector sources such as universities, polytechnics, research councils and government research establishments. It offers to take responsibility for protecting and licensing inventions from these sources, provides funds for development, seeks licensees and negotiates licence agreements with industry.

As part of its technology transfer role, BTG also offers project finance to companies that want to develop new products and processes based on new technology. Through its joint venture finance, BTG can provide up to 50 per cent of the funds required and will expect to recover its investment by means of a percentage levy on sales of the resulting product or process. This finance is available to companies of all sizes, including subsidiaries.

BTG is not a grant-giving body. It seeks to make a return on its investments and approaches every transaction on a commercial basis.

It currently has a portfolio of 1860 inventions, over 600 licensees in Britain and overseas, 360 development projects at universities and other public sector institutions and 230 projects with industrial companies.

In cases where a particular technology requires the setting up of a new company, BTG can perform a catalytic role in launching start-up companies.

THE CHARTERED INSTITUTE OF PATENT AGENTS, Staple Inn Buildings, High Holborn, London WC1V 7PZ (01–405–9450). Contact: M. C. Ralph. Provides booklets on patents, trademarks and designs, together with the Register of Patent Agents, which lists all UK patent agents entitled to practice in these fields. These agents advise on all forms of protection for ideas or manufactured goods, will act as the legal representative for obtaining this protection and will be able to assist with litigations to enforce the protection granted.

THE INSTITUTE OF INVENTORS, 19 Fosse Way, Ealing, London W13 OBZ (01–998–3540/4372). Contact: M. V. Rodrigues. The emphasis of the Institute's work is to help private inventors at all stages of their invention (e.g. sifting, appraising, advice on patenting, raising finance, sale of licenses and guidance to available government schemes or grants). It also provides a 'patenting service' including the preparation of drawings and specifications.

THE INSTITUTE OF PATENTEES AND INVENTORS, Staple Inn, Buildings' South, 335 High Holborn, London WC1V 7PX (01–242–7812). The Institute gives guidance and advice to members on all aspects of inventing.

P.A. PATCENTRE INTERNATIONAL, Cambridge Division, Melbourn, Royston, Herts SG8 6DP (0763–61222). The role of this body is to help to develop products for companies which will be commercially successful.

---

[1] One of the more comprehensive sources of information for new and small businesses is Colin Barrow's *The Small Business Guide* (British Broadcasting Corporation, 1984) which contains about 400 pages of useful information on a whole range of relevant topics.

PRUTEC, 17 Buckingham Gate, London SW1E 6LN (01–828–2082). PRUTEC is a subsidiary of Prudential Assurance which seeks investment opportunities in technological innovation. It has close links with P.A. International and in addition to providing investment finance gives technological and commercial advice as well.

Q.M.C. INDUSTRIAL RESEARCH LTD, 229 Mile End Road, London E1 4AA (01–790–0066). Contact: H. L. Roberts. Q.M.C. Industrial Research Ltd is a wholly owned company of Queen Mary College, University of London, which makes available the invention expertise and equipment of the college to industry. It has available highly qualified staff, equipment and supporting technicians in the fields of biology, chemistry, computer science, physics, materials science, mathematics, geography, earth science, and aeronautical, civil, electrical, mechanical and nuclear engineering. The objects of the company are to bring university research to bear on industrial problems, to stimulate academic research by contact with industries which are leading to technological change, and to do these things profitably so that the total potential for innovation is increased.

TECHNOLOGY ADVISORY POINT, Ebury, Bridge House, 2/18 Ebury Bridge Road, London SW1W 2QD (01–730–9678). Contact: I. Melville. The objective of TAP is to help UK industry to increase its profitability by providing R & D expertise, not only from its own research establishments but also by providing detailed information on the facilities and developments in other associations and academic institutions. Its aim is to provide a single point of contact for businesses which are facing technological problems and require the opportunity to discuss these with qualified staff.

TECHNOLOGY POLICY UNIT, Department of Industry, 29 Bressenden Place, London SW1E 5DT (01–213–5433). Contact: Dr R. Wiggins. Set up to provide support for innovation, the TPU offers advice and help in several areas including: computer-aided design and computer-aided manufacturing, flexible manufacturing systems, fibre optics, microelectronics, the application of industrial robots and the promotion of computer softwear products and packages.

THE DESIGN COUNCIL, 28 Haymarket, London SW1Y 4SU (01–839–8000). The Council's role is to advise on product design and to help in the investigation of technical problems for existing products. It has four regional offices at the following addresses:

The Design Council: Scottish Design Centre, 72 St Vincent Street, Glasgow G2 5TN (041–221–6121).

The Design Council: Design Centre Wales, Pearl Assurance House, Greyfriars Road, Cardiff CF1 3JN (0222–395–811).

The Design Council: Midlands, Norwich Union House, 31 Waterloo Road, Wolverhampton WV1 4BP (0902–773631).

The Design Council: Northern Ireland, Windsor House, 30 Victoria Street, Belfast BT1 3GS (0232–338452).

Appendix 2: Research and technology organisations

There are many research organisations which can provide help and information on those products or ideas which fall within their sphere of interest. Most are affiliated to the Association of Independent Research and Technology Organisation (AIRTO), c/o BHRA, Cranfield, Bedford MK43 OAJ. (0234–750422). The list is extensive but should you not appear to be able to match your needs with the listing then contact those who seem the nearest fit or the Department of Trade and Industry who may be able to advise.

THE ADVANCED MANUFACTURING TECHNOLOGY RESEARCH INSTITUTE, Hulley Road, Macclesfield, Cheshire SK10 2NE (0625–25421). Contact: L. K. Lord. Turnover £1.1m with a staff of 65. Activities and capabilities include consultancy, design (inclucing CAD), development, applications engineering, performance evaluation and development, problem-solving and information and advisory services in the mechanical, electrical, electronic, production and manufacturing fields, including AMT, for the designers, manufacturers and users of machine tools, and the designers and manufacturers of other forms of machinery.

BICERI – THE BRITISH INTERNAL COMBUSTION ENGINE RESEARCH INSTITUTE LIMITED, 111–112 Buckingham Avenue, Slough SL1 4PH (0753–27371). Contact: I. A. C. Brown. Turnover £2.0m with a staff of 75. Activities and capabilities include research, development and consultancy service to reciprocating internal combustion engine and component manufacturers and users, oil and additive companies and government departments covering a wide range of engines from road vehicles to marine diesels.

BCIRA, Alvechurch, Birmingham B48 7QB (0527–66414). Contact: I. C. H. Hughes. Turnover £2.7m with a staff of 140. Activities and capabilities include contract research, consultancy and technical advisory services to the foundry industry and associated industries worldwide. Expertise and experience in cast iron and other cast ferrous and non-ferrous metals, foundry design and organisation, melting, molten metal treatment, properties of castings, plant engineering, moulding and coremaking, working environment, operating efficiency, control, instrumentation, NDT and pollution control.

BRITISH CERAMIC RESEARCH LIMITED (Ceram Research), Queen's Road, Penkhull, Stoke-on-Trent, ST4 7LQ (0782–45431). Contact: Dr D. W. F. James. Turnover £3.9m with a staff of 253. Activities and capabilities include research, development and testing in all areas of ceramics including whitewares, refractories, building materials, (bricks, clay pipes, calcium silicate bricks and tiles); high-tech ceramics; pigments and wall and floor tiles. Also undertakes chemical physical and micro-structural testing and structural masonry research.

BRITISH CLOTHING CENTRE, Clayton Wood Rise, Leeds LS16 6RF (0532–741526) Contact: Paul O'Brien. Turnover £0.50m with a staff of 22. Management consultancy specialising in the clothing industry. Activities and capabilities include manufacturing consultancy, systems, training technical audits of industrial performance, technology of the fabric/making-up interface and computers applications.

BRITISH GLASS INDUSTRY RESEARCH ASSOCIATION, Northumberland Road, Sheffield S10 2UA (0742–686201). Contact: P. J. Doyle. Turnover £0.65m with a staff of 43. The Association undertakes co-operative and privately sponsored research related to glass production, technology and applications. Consultative, testing and information services are available in the following fields: energy utilisation, furnaces, air pollution, noise measurement, refractories, glass melting and processing, chemical analysis, fracture analysis, expert witness and forensic examinations.

BHRA, THE FLUID ENGINEERING CENTRE, Cranfield, Bedford MK43 0AJ (0234–750422). Contact: I. Cooper. Turnover £4.7m with a staff of 200. BHRA is an independent, international centre providing high-quality technical solutions and troubleshooting services covering the fluid engineering problems experienced by a wide range of industries including: processing, manufacturing, oil, gas, petro-chemical, mining, defence, construction and civil engineering, and transport.

BRITISH LEATHER CONFEDERATION, Leather Trade House, Kings Park Road, Moulton Park, Northampton NN3 1JD (0604–494131). Contact: R. L. Sykes. Turnover £0.8m with a staff of 52. The British Leather Confederation offers comprehensive research and development facilities, statistical information and advice on training and health & safety. As the former BLMRA, which it embodies, the BLC can offer a wide range of technical services, including evaluation of leather and tanning chemicals and detailed information on effluent treatment.

BUILDING SERVICES RESEARCH AND INFORMATION ASSOCIATION, Old Bracknell Lane West, Bracknell, Berkshire RG12 4AH (0344–426511). Contact: Dr D. P. Gregory. Turnover £1.8m with a staff of 85. Activities include the provision of information, research, testing and consultancy to the heating, ventilating, air conditioning, plumbing and electrical services industry.

CIRIA, 6 Storey's Gate, London SW1P 3AU (01–222–8891). Contact: M. D. Hodgkinson (Company Secretary). Turnover £1.5m with a staff of 40. CIRIA is an association of Member organisations which carries out research into all aspects of construction. It manages and publicises research which is initiated and guided by its Members who have preferential access to the results. The cost of research is met from Member funds, special contributions and public funds.

CUTLERY AND ALLIED TRADES RESEARCH ASSOCIATION, Henry Street, Sheffield S3 7EQ (0742–769736). Turnover £0.16m with a staff of 12. Activities include research and development, testing and consultancy for the cutlery, machine knife, hand tool, holloware, surgical instrument industries, into areas such as metallurgy, corrosion, forming of light products in metal, cutting edge technology, applications of advanced technology, abrasive operations, development of quality standards and testing of cutlery, hacksaw blades, surgical implants and electro deposits.

ERA TECHNOLOGY LIMITED, Cleeve Road, Leatherhead, Surrey KT22 7SA (0372–374151). Contact: Dr A. W. Rudge. Turnover £9.3m with a staff of 375. Provides services in electronic and electrical engineering, materials science and radio frequency technology, from market research through to research development and design with comprehensive laboratory testing, workshop and fabrication facilities.

FABRIC CARE RESEARCH ASSOCIATION, Forest House Laboratories, Knaresborough Road, Harrogate, Yorkshire HG2 7LZ (0423–883201). Contact: Dr R. M. Neale. Turnover £0.6m with a staff of 40. Activities and capabilities include the technology of laundering, dry cleaning and textile rental with particular reference to machine design and utilisation, performance of textile assemblies, the chemistry of liquid cleansing processes and all aspects of plant management and control of utilities consumption.

FULMER RESEARCH INSTITUTE LIMITED, Hollybush Hill, Stoke Poges, Slough, Berkshire SL2 4QD (02816–2181) Contact: Dr W. E. Duckworth. Turnover £4.9m with a staff of 243. Provides a range of services including product design and process development activities using advanced materials technology, market evaluation, technical consultancy, new materials development, testing, certification, quality assurance and design audit.

FURNITURE INDUSTRY RESEARCH ASSOCIATION, Maxwell Road, Stevenage, Hertfordshire, SG1 2EW (0438–313433). Contact: A. D. Spillard. Turnover £1.8m with a staff of 85. FIRA provides contract research, testing, technical, management and marketing services for furniture manufacturers and related industries, retailers, specifiers and suppliers of materials to the industry. Furniture design and development, factory planning, trouble shooting faults and computer systems advice. Testing and evaluation of all materials used by the industry and complete designs for strength and durability.

HAZLETON UK, Otley Road, Harrogate, North Yorkshire HG3 1PY (0423–500011). Contact: B. Cass. Turnover £5.6m with a staff of 250. Activities include product safety evaluation in the life sciences and research support across a range of related services and products to meet requirements of regulatory authorities worldwide.

HATRA, THE KNITTING CENTRE, 7 Gregory Boulevard, Nottingham NG7 6NB (0602–623311). Contact: J. P. Harrison. Turnover £0.36m with a staff of 18. Services include management consultancy, quality assurance, productivity studies, testing, training and video production research for the knitting and associated industries.

INTERNATIONAL RESEARCH AND DEVELOPMENT COMPANY LTD, Fossway, Newcastle-upon-Tyne NE6 2YD (091–2650451). Contact: S. Robson. Turnover £5.2m with a staff of 304. Activities include contractual research, development, prototype design/production, testing, technical support and consultancy services in the areas of mechanical, electrical and electronic engineering and materials technology.

INVERESK RESEARCH INTERNATIONAL LIMITED, Musselburgh, EH21 7UB, Scotland (031–665–6881). Contact: Dr I. P. Sword. Turnover £6m with a staff of 250. Provides research in toxicology, mutagenicity, biotechnology, metabolic studies and clinical trials, thrombosis research and analytical chemistry.

LAMBEG INDUSTRIAL RESEARCH ASSOCIATION, The Research Institute, Lisburn, County Antrim, N. Ireland BT27 4RJ (084–62–2255). Contact: I. T. Hamilton. Turnover £0.65m with a staff of 65. Activities include research into long-staple textiles, (especially flax), linen, linen blends, polyolefins. Also involved in environmental pollution, specialising in low-cost catalysts tailored for use with specific liquid or gaseous materials and flammability including the development of flame retardants.

LIFE SCIENCE RESEARCH LIMITED, Eye, Suffolk IP23 7PX (0379–4122). Contact: Dr K. H. Harper. Turnover £9.0m with a staff of 420. Engaged in contract research and consultancy in life sciences with special reference to toxicity and general safety evaluation, consumer product testing, clinical assessment, regulatory affairs and product registration.

MOTOR INDUSTRY RESEARCH ASSOCIATION, Watling Street, Nuneaton, Warwickshire CV10 0TU (0203–348541). Contact: Dr C. Ashley. Turnover £6.6m with a staff of 249. MIRA covers every aspect of vehicle technology, safety, emissions, performance, dynamics, durability, acoustics, aerodynamics, stress analysis, ergonomics, engines, braking, transmission, computing, electronics, electro-magnetic compatibility, computer-aided design, civil and mechanical facility design and consultancy. It also offers a design development and research service to vehicle manufacturers and component suppliers world-wide.

NATIONAL COMPUTING CENTRE LIMITED, Oxford Road, Manchester, M1 7ED (061–228–6333). Contact: E. Scriven. Turnover £10.8m with a staff of 394. The NCC provides public and in-house training courses and produces a wide range of training materials for sale or hire. It supplies software packages, publishes books and offers a variety of information and consultancy services.

PAINT RESEARCH ASSOCIATION, 8 Waldegrave Road, Teddington, Middlesex, TW11 8LD (01–977–4427). Contact: J. A. Bernie. Turnover £0.75m with a staff of 60. Provides research, analysis, consultancy, testing, information services and training relating to the manufacture and use of paints and other surface coatings.

PERA (PRODUCTION ENGINEERING RESEARCH ASSOCIATION), Melton Mowbray, Leicester, LE13 0PB (0664–501501). Contact: R. A. Armstrong. Turnover £16.7m with a staff of 350. Provides industrial research, development and consultancy in the main areas of advanced manufacturing technology, design, materials engineering, electronics and computer software, production technology and industrial marketing and promotions. Membership services include database and library access, technical enquiry service and technical translations.

PIRA (PAPER AND BOARD, PRINTING AND PACKAGING INDUSTRIES RA), Randalls Road, Leatherhead, Surrey KT22 7RU (0372–376–161). Contact: B. W. Blunden. Turnover £4.6m with a staff of 180. PIRA is the technical centre for the paper, printing and packaging industries with an annual R & D budget of £1.5m.

PROCESSORS AND GROWERS RESEARCH ORGANISATION, The Research Station, Great North Road, Thornhaugh, Peterborough PE8 6HJ (0780–782585). Contact: G. P. Gent. Offers an advisory service on all aspects of production of peas and beans including husbandry, economic value of crops, choice of variety for specific markets and areas, harvesting, drying, and weed, pest, disease and disorder problems. Full laboratory service are available for the identification of pests and diseases.

RAPRA TECHNOLOGY LTD, Shawbury, Shrewsbury, Shropshire SY4 4NR (0939–250383). Contact: Dr M. M. Hall. Turnover £2.9m with a staff of 156. Provides scientific, technological, information, commercial and marketing services for the rubber and plastics industries, their suppliers, and the end-users of their products.

SHIPOWNERS REFRIGERATED CARGO RESEARCH ASSOCIATION, 140 Newmarket Road, Cambridge CB5 8HE (0223–65101). Contact: G. R. Scrine. Turnover £0.3m with a staff of 13. Engages in research into the storage and transport by sea and land of perishable foodstuffs and other commodities. This includes heat transfer, temperature control and monitoring including microprocessor applications. Heat pumps and refrigeration systems for containers and road transport vehicles. Also provide thermal testing of equipment including vehicles and containers, air distribution systems and fan performance.

SPRING RESEARCH AND MANUFACTURERS' ASSOCIATION, Henry Street, Sheffield S3 7EQ (0742–760771). Contact: J. A. Bennett. Turnover £0.35m with a staff of 20. SRAMA undertakes a co-operative research programme and contract research into all aspects of spring technology including materials evaluation; design, manufacturing processes; corrosion protection; software development; and statistical process control.

STEEL CASTINGS RESEARCH AND TRADE ASSOCIATION, 5 East Bank Road, Sheffield S2 3PT (0742–28647). Contact: J. R. Whitehead. Turnover £1.9m with a staff of 95. SCRATA operates both a trade and a research division. Membership of the trade division is restricted to UK steelfounders. The research division undertakes research and promotes sales of plant to transfer technology to members. Information is freely available to members and users of steel castings.

TIMBER RESEARCH AND DEVELOPMENT ASSOCIATION, Stocking Lane, Hughenden Valley, High Wycombe, Buckinghamshire HP14 4ND (0240–243091). Contact: R. T. Allcorn. Turnover £2.5m with a staff of 130. TRADA undertakes research and development to ensure the efficient and economic use of timber. Its services range from architectural consultancy, engineering design and timber component testing to quality assurance, fire tion dissemination is through publications, videos and a regional/advisory service, public relations activities, seminars and educational and training courses.

WATER RESEARCH CENTRE, Henley Road, Medmenham, Marlow, Buckinghamshire SL7 2HD (0491–571531). Contact: M. J. Rouse. Turnover £17.1m with a staff of 567. WRC is the UK's principal research organisation for water services. Its work includes drinking water treatment and quality, water supply and distribution, sewerage, sewage treatment, sludge treatment and disposal, freshwater quality, marine quality, environmental standards, legislation and compliance. Its consultancy and specialist services are handled through its subsidiary WRC Contracts Ltd.

WIRA TECHNOLOGY GROUP LTD, Wira House, West Park Ring Road, Leeds LS16 6QL (0532–781381). Contact: Dr B. E. King. Turnover £2.4m with a staff of 120. Wira Technology Group is an independent organisation serving the wool textile and allied industries and also many other sectors. Services include R & D, consultancy, testing, arbitration, information technology, training and instrument manufacture. Specialist expertise covers such topics as textile processing and performance, carpets, energy, water and effluent, noise, engineering, chemical analysis, and surface cleaning and maintenance.

CHAPTER 5

Defining and Determining Capacity

Need for a planned approach to capacity

'Capacity' in this chapter is defined broadly as the major capital or fixed assets of a business – the buildings, land, plant and equipment. Decisions to commit relatively large proportions of plant and the limited resources of a small business in buying capacity need to be treated with great care. Small business ventures are extremely vulnerable; they are rarely able to hedge their judgements in the area of investment decisions. This is, however, an area where very often decisions are taken intuitively – often almost as an act of faith. There can be a feeling that investment in capacity is essential to support growth, to increase competitiveness, and consequently to increase market share. It can be assumed that this is the way to make your cash work for the business. Through more conservative eyes, the picture looks very different. Investment in capacity has an inevitable timescale, implies specific commitments, reduces options, and ties up cash. It makes a fundamental impact on what can and what cannot be done in terms of **organising the production/operations processes.**

'Capacity' is also a decision area where funds can often be more easily made available. Banks are generally keen to increase their own loan stock; government departments have special grants available for the purpose; local councils are often willing to fund the early years in order to attract more businesses (and therefore jobs) to an area; EEC funds are available and there are also a growing range of options in terms of the type of readily available capacity provided by industrial estates, business parks, science parks, and so on.

The spur from central government is to encourage new businesses and the figures, in part, support this. In the period from June 1981 to September 1982, over 8,000 loans (totalling in excess of £250 million) were made under the Loan Guarantee Scheme of which 50 per cent were for new businesses.[1] 'So', concludes John Edwards, 'the new rules of the game allow for an easy birth'.[2] He goes on to say, however, that of those businesses 'the vast majority will stay small whilst some will thrive on low overheads, fast response times and high energy or commitment. To the liquidator, however, the rules of the game have not changed and the penalties of failure remain the same. The diversity of choice offered for new starters is high, but the track record is low and unprofessional'.

In fact, the opportunities for new start-ups are in some ways remarkable – easy availability of start-up funds, plenty of advice and government encouragement – but the environment and the economy provide a tough testing ground. New entrants are not, for the most part, entering with new ideas, new technologies and new skills. They are entering an already congested market, with many companies already in the field experiencing declining profitability.

These words are stark, but so are the facts. **Four out of every five start-ups fail.** To avoid this it is important, therefore, to plan well at all levels. This requires more objective analysis and avoidance of the

[1] Robson Rhodes Report (1983, pp. 22–3).
[2] Edwards, 1983.

pitfalls associated with closed minds and subjective judgements. The difficulty, however, is largely an 'attitude problem' rather than one of insurmountable obstacles. The approaches to capacity planning in this chapter, and the methodologies outlined in the following ones, are not difficult in themselves. The hard work is being **more systematic about the major decisions facing the business** and being able to apply yourself to the task. Working effectively against the wrong plan – particularly the wrong investment plan – will bring scant reward. Whilst luck will always play its part, sound planning will substantially reduce the risk of failure and provide the essential guidelines in both start-up and growth situations.

It is often tempting to rationalise 'success' and 'failure' in terms of luck. Remember, however, that sound planning and luck are not without their links. What planning will give you is the wherewithal to **make the best of the opportunities which come your way.**

A framework for capacity planning

Before moving into the methodology and technologies necessary for effective capacity planning there are a number of general points which need to be set out to provide a framework for the planning process. Changes in capacity have significant effects on the fundamental character of, the options available to, and the operations management tasks within, a business. We can give five examples where changes in capacity will have tangible effects on the business, and these can be anticipated and generally quantified:

1. **Effects on business options**. The need to recognise that the type of capacity provided influences the **strategic and operational options** available to a business.

2. **Effects on product and services**. Products and services will change (usually **incrementally**) over a period of time and capacity decisions can either inhibit, absorb or even facilitate these changes.

3. **Effects on operational costs and overheads**. Investment in capacity also generates **overheads** which must be recovered.

4. **Effects on production/operations control**. The increased capacity will often result in increased **complexity in the control and information systems** required to arrange and manage the production/operations function.

5. **Effects on the POM task**. Capacity decisions significantly affects the **POM** task in terms of its size and nature.

Effects on business options

A 'press tools' business, limited to the capacity of the owner's garage has a very different range of business options available when compared to a competitor with cheap, purpose-built space on a local industrial estate. The corner shop hemmed in by other housing has a different range of opportunities available compared with the neighbouring self-service shop which has plenty of space for display and customers' shopping trolleys. The motor vehicle mechanic who operates from a 'mobile' workshop is offering a very different service to the local Ford 'main agent' garage, and has a different range of business options available.

These are self-evident statements, presenting very obvious differences. Most capacity decisions, however, are more subtle and reflect more complex sets of options or trade-offs. In this sense capacity decisions need to be based very much on a scenario of the type of business which the owner/manager **wants now and that which he or she aspires to develop**. The absence of this link back into the owner/manager's personal strategies for the business is likely to lead to inappropriate capacity decisions, in terms of both fit and timing.

Effects on products and services

Products and services will change over a period of time – the problem is that these are generally slow, incremental changes. The product life cycle concept is one which always operates. The key is to anticipate the **nature and timescale of the changes** in product and services. Then one must determine whether capacity should be chosen with the flexibility to accommodate changes, or whether the business needs to accept that existing capacity will also have a limited usefulness and ensure that it does not become a millstone. In many businesses, this will mean a decision on new products and services.

Effects on operational costs and overheads

The type of capacity and the type of capital or fixed assets available to a business substantially affect its operational costs – generally, the greater the capacity, the greater the operational costs. The benefits of increased capacity – economics of scale, increased throughput, lower process costs wider range of processes, products or services, etc. – need to be **identified** and the economies weighed in terms of competitiveness, market penetration, sales/volume, increased opportunities, and so on, in both the short and long term. Usually, however, the initial increases in capacity can bring a disproportionate increase in overhead costs while the business is building up towards its potential. During this period, funds need to be available to 'buffer' the business until the 'payback' period arrives.

In many small businesses, costs which are deemed to be variable often contain large elements which are, in fact, **fixed**. A good example of this is the short-term difficulty of reducing (or effectively using elsewhere) 'excess' capacity brought on by a reduction in demand. Direct labour is difficult to shed immediately due to the uncertainty about future capacity needs and the legal responsibilities of an employer. Machine capacity may similarly be (and often is) impractical to use on other products.

Overheads are an increasingly important element of total costs. In a review of the make-up of total costs in 10 separate small businesses it was revealed that whilst direct labour as a percentage of total costs ranged from 8 to 20, overheads averaged over 40 per cent with a high of 56 per cent.

The arbitrary allocation of overheads and the bases used to absorb them usually amount at best however, to crude accounting mechanisms. It is important that these methods are understood and their relevance challenged on a regular basis in order to avoid drifting into a situation where the allocation of the largest part of total costs is on an entirely arbitrary basis whilst the smallest (i.e., labour) is, as is the usual situation, expressed to two decimal places of a penny and with all the implied accuracy that accrues from such a cost statement.

Effects on production/operations control

Controls, procedures, technical know how and support are some of the many important infrastructure changes which go hand-in-hand with capacity changes. If they do not have direct cost implications, they will certainly add to the size of the control task, demand adjustments to procedures, require additional technical support, and so on. Each of these takes up management time and effort – costly in itself and normally diverting attention from other, equally important, tasks. The failure fully to appreciate all the consequences involved, together with both the stepped or incremental nature that such changes will have on a business can often lead to major problems.

The hardware requirements to meet capacity and capability changes in a business are normally readily recognised, and the arguments understood by all concerned. However, when additional investment is proposed to provide the necessary support for (or to meet the increasing complexity brought on by) such changes over time, many businesses will tend either to argue away these needs or to question why the existing control systems (and other aspects of the infrastructure) cannot cope. In small businesses particularly, where infrastructure provision is usually less than it is in a large-sized company, the need to recognise this problem is even more important. Where additional investment in procedures, controls and the like or the increase in overhead costs cannot be met, then a critical POM task is to review the current roles, procedures, controls and sets of re-sponsibilities which exist and, in the light of the revised requirement, decide **where the priorities lie.**

Effects on the POM task

Capital and capacity investment decisions will, quite properly, focus mainly on the costs associated with buildings/plant/equipment/ process decisions. It is important, however, for a small business to realise that, in addition, the **POM task will be affected by those same decisions.** The nature of these latter changes will be of a more intangible nature and, though acknowledged, rarely forms part of the total decision and is usually treated as a 'consequential' issue.

A business faced, for example, with the decision on how to re-spond to supplying a new product involving several components which need to be assembled has several capacity-related options – all of which affect the POM task in fundamentally different ways. If they opt for a wholly made-in-house approach they will need capacity (buildings, equipment, and processes) which can accommodate a wide process span – this will, however, imply consequential POM issues which need to be considered. If, however, it was felt that investment in capacity needed to be kept to an absolute minimum level they may choose to reduce dramatically the in-house process span, concentrating only on final assembly and packaging – all components and sub-assemblies being produced by various sub-contractors. This 'capacity and process span' decision produces a totally different set of POM tasks – requiring different sets of skills, structures, resources, planning and control systems, compared with the wholly 'made-in' decision. It will require a good supplies function capable of liaising with a number of sub-contractors, appropriate in-house engineering provision (including support for suppliers and quality control checks in line with external supply), and very simple in-house assembly planning and control tasks.

Capacity planning

This chapter has so far stressed the importance of planning present and future capacity requirements. Not only does this involve the translation of demand forecasts into process and labour requirements but it also involves decisions on whether to provide this **ahead of or in reaction to actual orders.** (i.e. to lead or follow demand). The steps involved start with these tasks which have the longer time periods and move backwards to the control of day-to-day operations. Even though many businesses experience great difficulty in projecting forward through forecasts they do in fact make capacity decisions of both a short- and longer-term nature. The degree to which these decisions are intuitive or based more on analysis will vary from one business to another. There is, however, a clear and well-tried methodology or sequence of steps which relates to long-term capacity planning. If this is understood and applied a business is able to move from informal, intuitive decision-making to more rational capacity decisions, which will lead to improved business control, reduce the need for unplanned expansions and lessen the risk of having spare, unusable capacity. The main steps are:

1. Forecast **demand**.
2. Decide whether to '**make**' or '**buy**'.
3. Examine '**size of plant**' issues.
4. Identify the **customer's role** in capacity provision.
5. Define the **production/provision plan**.

Forecasting demand

Market research and sales forecasting will be dealt with at much greater length in the marketing book in this series.[1] However, as the conversion of the forecasts into capacity requirements is the starting point for the business plan, it is important to say a little about forecasting and how it affects the POM task.

All forecasts by definition are inaccurate (even so, crude estimates are usually better than none at all). The reason for this inaccuracy is that there are two dimensions of a demand forecast: **a statement of magnitude** (which relates to the long-term capacity planning aspects) and **a statement of detail** (which relates more to the production planning and operational control aspects). The former relates to the global size of sales whilst the latter consists of statements of planned

---

[1] Derek Waterworth, *Marketing for the Small Business* (Macmillan, 1987).

sales for individual products/services. Whilst the latter is often the constituent of the former, the characteristics of these two dimensions are not the same.

As the forecast statement becomes more global, for example, the chances of it being 'wrong' reduce. The more detailed the forecast becomes and the shorter the timescale involved then the less reliable it is likely to be. The danger, however, is that the increased level of detail often implies greater reliability – a point touched on previously.

The POM task, however, is to meet not only total capacity requirement but also the sales of individual items. Planning at the broad level is thus required to ensure both that total capacity provision is met (the subject of this chapter) and that the changing demand for individual sales is also effectively scheduled (the subject of Chapter 6.) There is a need, therefore, to test forecasts and check their inherent accuracy. This may include (a) determining the **level of risk or certainty or confidence** of the forecast (don't accept one-figure forecasts); (b) testing the apparent detail against the timescale and identify any **assumptions**; and (c) ensuring that there is an appropriate 'rationale' or logic **linking the global to the detailed forecasting statement**. Consolidating several detailed product forecasts into a global capacity plan, for example, involves ensuring that the timescale base of the final global plan (often two years or more) is not simply derived from last year's monthly sales schedules.

'Make or buy' decisions

In theory, every part of a product/service is a candidate either for manufacture/provision in-house or for buying from an external supplier. In reality, it will be found when reviewing this decision that with certain items in the product/service mix there is only one sensible choice to be made. We can now look at some of the important factors which must be taken into account when taking the decision to 'make in' or 'buy out'.

1. **The business**. Fundamental questions which need to be reviewed in the make or buy decision include 'what is the business really good at?', or 'what is it that makes the business unique?', or 'what is the business really selling?' The answer to these questions will help clarify the **essence of the business and hence the key aspect(s)** of manufacturing/provision **which must be retained inside**.

2. **Protection of ideas**. In a similar way, it is important to consider those aspects of your products/services which form the essence of what makes your product/service ideas **different to those of the**

competition. The protection of these ideas forms an important part of the make or buy decision.

3. **Capability and availability**. A specific consideration involved in the make or buy decision concerns whether or not you have the **internal capability** (see also the discussion on costs below) and whether suitable **suppliers** are available.

4. **Costs**. Cost is frequently the most important determining factor in the 'make or buy' question. However, it is most important to ensure that these decisions are based upon a **comparison of like with like**. Whereas the suppliers' quotations will be relatively cut and dried, it is important to remember these points:

- Does the outside price quotation include the same **cost constituents** as the internal estimates? One manufacturing company was proposing to buy from outside until it was pointed out that the outside supplier did not include initial tooling costs or tooling replacement. This made all the difference. Also, as shown earlier in the chapter, currently a large proportion of total costs consists of overheads. If the business cannot reduce those overheads associated with the product/services which it proposes to buy out, then the existing overheads should form part of both sets of cost.
- It is also most useful when making these comparisons to check if there is any relationship between the two sets of costs involved. In another manufacturing company it was found, when checking outside with inside costs, that the overhead content was the biggest area of difference (sufficiently accurate estimates of the material and labour content could be made in this instance). A review of the way these overhead costs were internally absorbed revealed that the overhead costs attributed to this range of products, due to the fact that a single absorption rate was being used, were disproportionately higher than with other products. As a result of this, the costing system was revised to reflect more accurately **real manufacturing costs** and to provide a sounder basis on which to make these critical, business decisions.
- The **capital investment implications** (new or used, bought or leased) need to be carefully analysed, not only in terms of the obvious expenditure involved but also in terms of the level of technical support which may have to be provided. This is because it is an integral part of the total investment, necessary to ensure the effective use of the processes – which underpin the costs calculations involved.
- You will also find that there are other sets of costs associated

with bought-out and made-in decisions. Both will require different forms of technical support (see the last point) and also involve **infrastructure requirements concerning procedures and controls**. It is most important to assess these aspects of the total costs involved (no matter how difficult it at first may seem) in order to ensure that the decision is based upon a total review of all the factors involved.

5. **Emotion**. Finally, a business may sometimes decide not to purchase from outside, based on the unsubstantiated, emotional view that no one can make it better or cheaper than itself. It is important to check that this is not the sole basis on which the make or buy decision finally rests.

Size of plants

Although this may not be an important factor for the very small business, at the upper levels of the definition of 'small' the deliberation on plant size will need to form part of the capacity decision. Although arguments supporting the economies of large scale have been made in the past, these are increasingly under scrutiny. The temptation to absorb growth on the same site is often high in a small business situation. However, a review of size on a regular basis should be made to ensure that the **incremental nature of growth** does not go unnoticed and unaccounted for.

Customers' role in capacity provision

One aspect which particularly concerns service businesses is defining the role of customers in terms of capacity provision. Because of the inherent product/customer interaction in a service business, **the consumer becomes a source of capacity**. The extent to which the consumer provides process capacity will vary according to the design of the service. Compare the role of customers in a self-service retail store or restaurant to their role in a counter service or waiter service business and the different impact it makes on capacity. In some manufacturing companies, the role of the customer needs to be thought through, for similar reasons. In one sub-contract company, the entrepreneur was intending to pick up and deliver from and to the customer. However, on reviewing the impact that this would have on capacity (and particularly his own time) he decided to provide a business on a set down/collect basis. Although, initially this may have lost him sales, in the end he was able to spend his time doing the type of work which comprised the essence of what his business 'sold' – **the fast turnround of customers' orders**.

The production/provision plan

The nature of the production/provision plan which the business adopts (e.g., chase demand, level demand or mixed plan) will have its impact on both capacity and delivery. The alternative production/operations provision plans are discussed more fully in Chapter 6, both in themselves and in relation to the capacity and delivery issues relevant to the POM task.

In summary, the long-term capacity requirements need to be assessed in the light of the business analyses, sales forecasts and make or buy decisions which will enable you to **translate future demand into capacity**. Decisions concerning aggregate capacity planning[1] which will be made on the basis of the production plan(s) to be adopted will also affect this decision.

In small businesses, however, the problems of growth will involve additional dimensions: the relative significance of capacity increases, the shortage of capital and the understandable dominance of the shorter-term considerations will bring additional pressures.

However, it is important to recognise that planning does not actually cost or commit the business to a course of action. This is not to say that time is not valuable. What it does is to stress that unless there is an awareness of the capacity implications of future plans then these cannot form part of the total business decision or alert you to the considerable problems which may arise in periods of fluctuating or steady growth.

Business location and premises selection

An important aspect of the capacity decision for any business is selecting the location of the business and the appropriate premises in which to house it. Not many ventures start up with ideal premises. Most are forced to compromise and more often than not they start in their own or someone else's spare room, garage or loft. From there, the business is nurtured through its crucial, early stages. Eventually, the business will grow to the point where the pressure is such that

---

[1] This procedure is explained in some detail in Chapter 6 and involves establishing the overall or aggregate capacity requirement for all products/services.

commercial premises need to be sought. It is this decision to which this section relates.

Although the location of the business should come before the selection of the premises, in reality firms often consider these together and (as at all stages in their growth) make compromises between one factor and another. Similarly, although each decision will be different to the next, there are a number of factors which should be reviewed, some important to all types of business, others important only to specific types.

A retailer or service business will want the firm in the midst of the market to be served. Manufacturers often face the problems of wider geographical markets, especially as the business grows. Sub-contractors, on the other hand, may be more akin to the retail example given earlier. In all cases you may initially select your business site on cost factors alone and not necessarily on factors in line with your anticipated needs. Financial constraints will often lead you to select somewhere near to where you currently live (to avoid high relocation costs) and at a size which reflects the cash available. There is no correct solution. However, using the factors discussed here will help evaluate the alternatives in a much more objective way and enable you to be more conscious of the trade-offs involved in your choice.

Due to the very different set of problems facing the firm setting up for the first time as opposed to one which has been in business for some time, the particular sets of issues facing the new start- up will be dealt with separately. The more general factors affecting location for existing business are then discussed.

Factors of location and premises selection – new start-ups

The initial location of a new start-up is, understandably, likely to be in the area where the entrepreneur is currently living. If immediate ambitions are limited, businesses are often started up in parallel with the owner's full-time job with another firm. In these circumstances the option to be anywhere but in or near your own home is usually excluded from the decision. A Department of Industry report by A. J. Beaumont[1] confirmed that many founders of businesses choose their first location in their local area (i.e., within about 30 minutes' travelling distance of their house) for a variety of reasons:[2]

---

[1] Beaumont, 1982.
[2] See also Department of Industry, 1980.

- Family and other close **personal ties**.
- Minimises the problems of **working long and unsocial hours**.
- A **second mortgage** on their home is often a major source of business capital in the initial development of the product/service.
- At a time of setting up a business they do not wish to incur the additional **costs of moving house**.
- There is, at the beginning, an inherent measure of **uncertainty** as to whether the business will be successful.

The report revealed that some 24 per cent of the founders started at home and another 55 per cent in small premises close to home.[1] The critical problem facing a new start-up is the **potential cost of failing**. Consequently, there is a strong desire to take on as few long-term commitments as possible. The typical premises required by a new firm are often as basic as a garage-type building or shell (sometimes smaller than 500 square feet) available on terms that permit the tenant to leave at short notice without undue financial difficulties or obligations.[2] The give:

1. Proximity to **local customers**, particularly as initial orders or initial demand will be on a local basis.
2. Proximity to **local, known labour resources**. Knowing where suitable labour sources of all kinds can be tapped is often very advantageous at the initial stages of a business.

Factors of location and premises selection – existing businesses

Whilst it is recognised that the initial choice of location will be a major influence on subsequent sites, it is important for a small business, as it develops and the initial fears about survival have begun to recede, to consider its **changing-location and premises-selection priorities**. It will help in doing this to consider the following factors, some of which probably formed part of the new start-up decision originally.

Market-related factors

There are two important market-related factors which need to be taken into account when selecting a suitable location. The first of these concerns **demand forecasts for the products or services**. If the

---

[1] Beaumont (1982, p. 7).
[2] This was one of the conclusions in Department of Industry (1980, Section 2, para. 2.12).

business is predominantly supplying the local community then a careful study of present and future sales potential must be completed. Different sites within each area will obviously bring higher sales, and this relationship of sales volume to location cost needs to be an important part of the total assessment.

It will be necessary to analyse the types of businesses and population make-up within each locality, as well as the alternative sites which are available and how well these relate to your own market needs. A comprehensive analysis should therefore include:

1. **Local businesses**
- Types, distinguished between **supportive** and **competitive**.
- The **relative density** and **geographical position** of these other businesses.
- The **level of diversification** which exists.
- The **degree of seasonality** within each business.
- The nature of the businesses in terms of whether they are **old, established, new, prospering or uncertain**.
- Trends in terms of **growth or decline** by business type.

2. **Population**
- **Income distribution**.
- **Living status**.
- **Age mix**.
- The **daily inflow or outflow** of people (both workers and customers).
- Trends in terms of **growth and decline, income, age and living status**.

3. **Premises**
- The site of **competitors** relative to your type of business, large companies/retail chains, surrounding business (e.g., the shops in the same parade or street).
- Number of **vacant sites**, size (estimated employees and sales) of your nearest competitor and other nearby businesses.
- **Physical and geographical factors**: access, bus stops, traffic flow (including pedestrians), parking availability and restrictions, frontage, depth of site, shape of building, entrances, display space, corner or other location.
- **Unfavourable characteristics**, for example, poor pavements, unsightly buildings close by, and levels of smoke, dust, odours, noise, from nearby local industry.
- **History** of the site.

4. Competition

- Number of **competing businesses**.
- **Type** (attractive, growing, well-established, declining).
- **Management** (progressive, alert, apparent level of ability).
- **Pressure from large, national businesses** (e.g., retail chain stores).
- Growth/decline in the size of businesses in the **past and the anticipated future trends**.

Cost-related factors

Costs will play an important part in any decision on premises. It is necessary, therefore, to consider **projected costs** in this assessment since, once established, the inertia and associated disturbance and costs will militate against relocation. Some of the important areas of cost to be taken into account are:

1. **Transportation**. The costs of transportation are currently high and will be an even more important aspect in the future. They involve supplier, customer, employee and sub-contracted services.

2. **Labour availability and cost**. Obviously the demand/supply relationship affects the cost of labour at all levels in the firm.

3. **Utilities**. The availability and associated cost of energy and other utilities is an important consideration, especially when projecting into the future.

4. **Site and buildings**. The cost of the site, required additional buildings or alterations and the potential for expansion and its associated costs are all important facts to be taken into account.

5. **Rent and rates**. The rent charge, local rates and other similar costs will form part of this decision.

6. **Assisted Area status**. The attraction of assisted areas or other special grants will need to form part of the total decision and the trade-offs involved with the other cost, market-related and social factors need to be carefully weighed up.

Social and other infrastructure factors.

The final aspects to be taken into account come under the broad heading of social and other infrastructure factors. These include:

1. **Provision of suitable premises**. The investigation undertaken for the Department of Industry on the provision of small industrial

premises concluded that 'a shortage of small industrial premises persists in the country as a whole'. It also stated that 'there is clear evidence that the shortage of units has constrained the establishment and development of small firms; the provision of premises on suitable terms has undoubtedly itself had the effect of stimulating the formation of new firms and the growth of existing small firms.[1] Based upon this evidence, one important location factor therefore, concerns the provision of premises on 'suitable terms' – i.e., those which do not impose a long-term commitment.[2]

2. **Housing and amenities**. The availability of housing and local amentities may, especially with a growing small business, become an increasingly important factor.

3. **Local regulations**. The local regulations relating to aspects such as safety, planning, building and pollution will often present difficulties to a business, especially at times of growth and diversification. It is, therefore, important to be aware of these and note any that may affect your current and future plans.

4. **Transport and car parking**. Local transport and the existence of suitable car parking will for some businesses be a critical factor in where to locate their business (e.g., retail shops and restaurants).

5. **Technical**. For many businesses it is most important that they are located within (or, at any rate, with easy access of) the necessary infrastructure support for their business (in terms of technical, purchasing, sub-contracting and other related support), as this forms an essential, ongoing business requirement.

6. **Science parks, innovation and technology centres**. Moves to encourage the growth of technical innovation have started in the UK in the form of the provision of science parks, innovation and technology centres. A study prepared for the Department of Industry and Shell UK Ltd[3] concluded that there are two main types of science parks and related schemes as a means of supporting small firms:

(a) High-quality, low-density developments catering for mobile R & D or high-technology projects of major companies, or for small but fast-growing advanced technology companies seeking to enhance their image and working environment, and national or other research institutions.

(b) Schemes offering 'incubator space' for high-technology projects.

Since the first science park opened in 1975 (based at Trinity College, Cambridge) several other parks, innovation and technology centres

---

[1] Department of Industry (1980, paras. 2.102 and 2.105, p. 27); the survey was concerned with provision only in England.
[2] Department of Industry (1980, pp. 14; 43).
[3] Department of Industry, 1982.

have (or are planned to be) opened in the UK. Brief details of these
are given at the end of the chapter (Appendix 1, page 99).

7. **Provision of conventional common services**. In the UK, schemes
have been started to provide the following conventional common services:

- **Office support**, including physical facilities (e.g., reception
  and conference room) and **administrative support** (e.g., telephone answering, mail handling and security provision).
- General **business advice**.
- **Machinery and equipment**, generally for prototype development purposes.

A detailed appraisal of seven such schemes plus a broad review of
many others and the principal findings made are provided in the
Department of Industry and Shell UK Ltd study.[1]

Layout of facilities

The way in which facilities, services, plant, equipment are laid out
within a site or premises has a significant effect on the production/
operations task, and is, therefore, an important part of capacity
planning.

Facilities layout is important at two levels: the general level, which
concerns the disposition of **departments and activity groups on a site**,
and the detailed level, which locates the position of facilities **within
each department or area**.

Types of layout

There are three broad types of layout which will relate to the choice of
process you have made (refer to Chapter 2):

1. **Fixed-position layout**. Due to the size or fixed nature of the
product (e.g., a building) or the fragile nature of the service (e.g., a
banquet/dinner provided in the home of your customer), the resources need to be taken to the site.

2. **Process layout**. This type of layout is characterised by physically
bringing together similar process capabilities. The reason for this is to
serve the needs of the process rather than the needs of individual

---

[1] Department of Industry, 1982.

products/services. Examples in manufacturing are where machines providing the same function (e.g., drilling machines and centre lathes) are located in the same geographical area. Similarly, a service organisation will often have different sections (e.g., invoice, sales and administration) in their own locations. In this way, the gains associated with balancing workloads, improved utilisation pooling expertise and sharing experience and ideas can be realised.

3. **Product/service layout**. The facilities in product/service layout are designed to try to **serve the needs of the product/service**. In this way the layout reflects the operations to be completed in providing an agreed range of products/services (e.g., an assembly line). To justify this dedication, the demand for the particular products/services will need to be very high.

Often firms when very small start with a product/service layout. The product/service range is very limited and hence it makes sense to reflect the product/service needs when positioning the plant. Furthermore, when an organisation is operating on a small scale, the people doing the work will tend to complete most (or all) of the operations involved. However, as the firm grows, jobs are broken down, process investment takes place and specialisation increases. In these circumstances, the needs of each set of processes will tend to become more important than any one product or service. Hence, the firm will move to a process layout. Finally, with further growth and high-volume requirements, many firms change parts of the layout to product or service layout due to the need to handle relatively high volumes on a low cost basis.

Steps in planning the physical facilities

1. **Determine the products/services to be provided**. The factors to be taken into account here include the make or buy decisions and the current and anticipated products/services to be provided.
2. Each product/service will need to be broken down into its **constituent parts** – this provides the basis for listing the operations (that is, the work to be done), the work movement and other activities necessary to complete the task on hand.
3. It is now necessary to determine **how long** it takes to perform each of the operations involved. The times can be used by selecting one of the appropriate ways of measuring work which are covered in Chapter 8.
4. The times obtained are then used to determine the **capacity requirements** in terms of both processes and people.

5. Having determined the capacity requirement, this will serve as the basis for establishing the other **non-processing facilities** which need to be accommodated. These include:

- The **support functions** (e.g., maintenance and administration).
- **Utilities** (e.g., water and energy).
- Other, **general facilities** (e.g., rest rooms, toilets and cloakrooms).
- **Stock or inventory holdings**.

6. The next step is to decide on the best arrangement for the main functions involved. This will provide a **general overall layout** for the site and will need to take into account the restrictions imposed by the existing building (e.g., points of access, walls, windows and any existing facilities). Some of the general points to be borne in mind in this decision are to achieve the maximum:

- **Flexibility**, so as to be able to respond quickly and effectively to meet future requirements without involving high costs.
- **Co-ordination** between departments and sections.
- **Use of space**.
- **Accessibility** for provisioning, servicing and maintenance.
- **Safety** for those at work.
- **Security** of the premises.
- **Facilitation** of the efficient movement of work, minimising handling and distances travelled.

To help achieve these aims, a **load or trip frequency chart** is used. With a matrix format similar to that shown in Figure 5.1, the various departments can be displayed and represent the origin (and destination) of movements between them. The actual movements can be determined through observation or from appropriate documents. If data does not exist, then estimates must be made. In addition, a **relationship chart** can be used (see Figure 5.2) to identify how close one department needs to be to another. This approach makes use of a priority code to show the preferred proximity of two departments and a justification code specifying the reason for the desired proximity. Preparing these types of charts will facilitate the preparation of a general overall layout by providing an **objective basis** on which to arrive at your decisions.

7. Next it is necessary to prepare alternative detailed layouts within a department. To do this the **sequence of operations involved to**

FROM \ TO	Departments								TOTAL
Departments	1	2	3	4	5	6	7	8	
1		28	–	–	16	43	5	9	101
2			19	–	6	2	–	18	45
3				2	12	7	–	28	49
4					–	15	58	–	73
5						13	21	17	51
6							6	38	44
7								–	–
8									
TOTAL	–	28	19	2	34	80	90	110	363

The bottom segment of this matrix is blank because in this instance the movements from, for example, Department 1 to Department 6 have been added to those movements from Department 6 to Department 1
If for any reason it was necessary to distinguish between these movements, then the chart can accommodate this

Source: Hill (1983, p. 98)

Figure 5.1   Load or trip frequency chart showing actual or simulated movements between departments

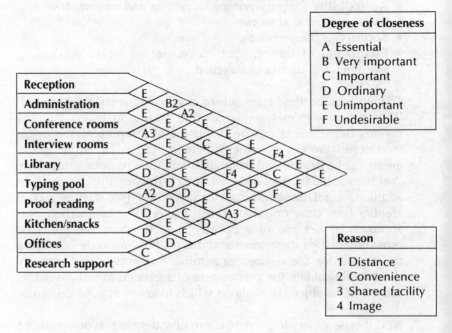

Degree of closeness

A Essential
B Very important
C Important
D Ordinary
E Unimportant
F Undesirable

Reason

1 Distance
2 Convenience
3 Shared facility
4 Image

Figure 5.2   Relationship chart for a small consultancy firm

complete each product/service will need to be established and reviewed. In most cases, this routing will form the basis of your layout.

8. It is important to remember, especially in the final two steps, to prepare **alternatives from which you can choose**, and also to **involve those concerned in the analysis and final decision**. In this way, you will not decide too early in the process and thereby be left with no choice at all. Also, you will benefit from the ideas and involvement of all those involved. This will make for a better solution and easier implementation and development of the chosen plan.

9. Finally it is essential to review **legislative considerations**, including, for example:

- Factories Act 1961 requires that each person should be allowed a minimum of **400 cubic feet** (the space in a room above the height of 14 feet is not included in this calculation and, where a room contains a gallery, the gallery shall be treated as a separate room).
- All layouts should be safe and include adequate **medical facilities, fire exits** (to be agreed with the local fire officer) **and gangways**.
- Adequate **lighting** needs to be provided and **noise levels** have to be kept within the required limits.

Appendix 1: Science/research parks, innovation and technology centres as a means of supporting small businesses

An increasing number of opportunities are being provided to help meet the needs of start-up businesses. Some of these provide only premises, whilst others offer encouragement and an environment which supports some of the needs of a small business. The late 1980s has seen a significant change in support provision for small companies compared to the help available even in the previous decade. Brief details on some of the science/research parks and innovation and technology centres, one example of this growing support, are given below.[1]

---

[1] See also Colin Barrow, *The Small Business Guide* (1984).

Science/research parks

ASTON SCIENCE PARK, Love Lane, Birmingham B7 4BJ (021–359–0981). Contact: B. Richards. Comprises about 20 acres, offering business units in the size range 35–500 square metres.

BIRCHWOOD SCIENCE PARK, Birchwood, Warrington, Cheshire (0925–51144). Contact: E. Bilton. Comprises about 75 acres, offering business units in the size range 50–5000 square metres.

BRUNEL SCIENCE PARK, Brunel University, Uxbridge, Middlesex (0895–39234). Contact: P. Russell. Comprises about 6.5 acres (with an additional 6.5 acres planned), offering business units in the size range 50–5500 square metres.

CAMBRIDGE SCIENCE PARK, Trinity College, Cambridge CB2 1TQ (0223–338400). Contact: Dr J. R. G. Bradfield. The Science Park itself is located in Milton Road, Cambridge (0223–861518). Comprises about 80 acres (with an additional 40 acres planned for the future), offering 65 business units in the size range 50 to 12 000 square metres.

MERSEYSIDE INNOVATION CENTRE, 131 Mount Pleasant, Liverpool L3 5TF (051–708–0123). Contact: B. Hollows/A. Rimmer. Comprises some 15 000 square feet, offering 12 business units in the size range 12–100 square metres.

PEEL PARK, East Kilbride Development Corporation, Atholl House, East Kilbride G74 1LK (03552–41111). Contact: A. Dalziel. Comprises 100 acres, offering to date 4 business units in the size range 1 000–3 000 square metres.

SURREY RESEARCH PARK, P. O. Box 112, University of Surrey, Guildford (0483–579693). Contact: Dr M. Parry. Comprises 70 acres (with a further 70 acres planned for the future), offering 23 business units (with 20 more available from mid-1987) in the size range 60–12 000 square metres.

UNILINK, Heriot Watt University, Riccarton, Edinburgh EH14 4AS (031–449–5111 or 031–226–6436). Contract: I. G. Dalton. A research park comprising 22 acres offering business units.

UNIVERSITY OF WARWICK SCIENCE PARK, Barclays Venture Centre, University of Warwick, Coventry CV4 7AL (0203–418535). Contact: D. N. E. Rowe. Comprises about 24 acres, offering 30 business units in the size range 40–3 000 square metres.

WEST OF SCOTLAND SCIENCE PARK, 101 Kelvin Campus, Glasgow G20 OSP (041–946–7161). Contact: A. McNicoll. Comprises about 62 acres, offering 36 business units in the size range 80–1 300 square metres.

Innovation centres

The National Association of Innovation Centres publishes a report which give details of their work and is available (price £6.00) from Dr K. Donaldson, Secretary, Association of Innovation Centre Executives, Hull Innovation Centre, Guildhall Road, Hull, HU1 1HJ. Information on some of the centres available throughout the UK is below.

Mr J. J. Downie
Industrial Development Unit
Strathclyde Regional Council
Strathclyde House 4
3 India Street
GLASGOW G2 4PF
041–227–3861

Dr J. Hedley
Tyne & Wear Innovation & Development Co Ltd
Green Lane Building
Heworth Way
Pelaw
GATESHEAD
Tyne & Wear NE10 OWW
091–438–2468

Dr K. Donaldson
Hull Innovation Centre
Guildhall Road
Queens Gardens
HULL HU1 1HJ
0482–226348

Mr P. Bissell
Calderdale Innovation Centre
Dean Clough Industrial Park
HALIFAX
W Yorkshire HX3 5AX
0422–42825

Mr A. Johnson
Industrial Development Unit
Telford Industrial Estate
Stafford Park 4
TELFORD
Shropshire TF3 3BA
0952–610329

Mr J. U. Shearn
Birmingham Innovation and Development Centre Ltd
Essex House
27 Temple Street
BIRMINGHAM B2 5DB
021–643–3430

Mr A. Kirby
Coventry Innovation Centre
Chamber of Commerce Building
St Nicholas Street
COVENTRY Warwickshire CV1 4FD
0203–662404 or 0203–51777

Mr K. Page
Welsh Development Agency
Treforest Industrial Estate
PONTYPRIDD
Mid-Glamorgan CF37 5UT
044–385 2666

Mr T. Libby
Cardiff and Vale Enterprise
5 Mount Square
CARDIFF CF1 6EE
0222–494411

Mr D. Patten
Somerset Innovation Centre
c/o CoSIRA
1 The Crescent
TAUNTON
Somerset
0823–76905

Mr B. Gills
Innovations Advisor
London Enterprise Agency
69 Cannon Street
LONDON EC4N 5AB
01–236–2675

Technology centres

BFIA TECHNOLOGY CENTRE, Shepherd Street, Sheffield S3 7BA
(0742–27463). Contact: Dr S. E. Rogers. Turnover £0.3m with a staff of 14.
Activities and capabilities include technology transfer to industries engaged
in the forming of solid metal. Technologies include forming processes,
mechanisation, computer-aided engineering, energy conservation, metallurgy and noise control.

BNF METALS TECHNOLOGY CENTRE, Grove Laboratories, Denchworth
Road, Wantage, Oxfordshire OX12 9BJ (02357–2992). Contact: Dr R. D.
Johnston. Turnover £2.4m with a staff of 112. Research, development and
consultancy carried out for world's metals industries. Specialisation is in
materials development, new process technology and management systems
for the production of semi-manufactures, castings and finished components,
and powder technology.

SATRA FOOTWEAR TECHNOLOGY CENTRE, Satra House, Rockingham Road, Kettering, Northamptonshire NN16 9JH (0536–516318). Contact: J. C. Bisson. Turnover £2.2m with a staff of 155. This centre has a membership of over 1000 in 20 countries. Its research and service activities cover all aspects of footwear technology, including material and component performance and use; manufacturing processes, machines and systems; production management, information systems, quality, health and safety control.

WHITECHAPEL TECHNOLOGY CENTRE, 75 Whitechapel Road, London (01–633–5380/01–633–5133). Contact: R. Willis/A. Hanman.

PART III

PRODUCTION/ OPERATIONS PLANNING AND CONTROL

CHAPTER 6

How to Plan and Control the Production/Operations System

Introduction

The five chapters which comprise Part III are concerned with providing an outline of the methodologies of analysis, planning and control of production/operations tasks. The aim of the business is to sell, profitably, its goods and services into its market. Success depends firstly on understanding how orders are won in that market, and secondly on evaluating how effectively the business can satisfy the order-winning criteria – generally this will be some combination of, for example, design, performance, quality, price and delivery speed. Achieving the necessary 'balance' between these performance criteria is heavily dependent on how well the **business plans and controls its production/operations functions**.

107

This 'internal' operations management task would be reasonably straightforward if the market demand was stable. A major difficulty is that **markets are inherently unstable**. When and how many products, or how much of a service, will be required is uncertain. Customers, whilst often giving an indication of the size of their likely demand, will order to meet their own needs rather than the needs of their suppliers. The 'ideal' conditions for the operations function to work most effectively is a totally stable or certain environment. In this situation it can plan and carry out its tasks in the most suitable way and organise them to suit its own internal needs. Unfortunately, the market place is far removed from this ideal. Consequently, a business has constantly to make trade-off decisions between the costs of the investment required to 'cushion' the impact of the unstable market on the operations processes and the costs associated with the impact of uncertainty on the requirements of the production/operations function. Some of the various options which can provide this 'cushioning' effect are considered in this chapter.

Levels of production/operations planning and control

The procedures used in the planning and control of the production/operations system vary in line with the time periods involved – the planning/control horizon will, in fact, vary from business to business. At the top end of the small business sector it will often range from day-to-day control to reviewing capacity needs five years or more in the future. At the lower end of the small business spectrum, looking any further than eighteen months or two years ahead (although desirable) is normally unrealistic. To help in distinguishing the tasks and procedures involved in this aspect of the business, it is useful to divide the planning horizon into three 'levels':

1. **Long-term operations planning**. This forms part of the capacity planning procedure covered in Chapter 5.
2. **Medium-term or aggregate planning**. This reviews the capacity needs of the business for up to two years ahead.
3. **Operations control**. This monitors the short-term activities involved in the production of goods or provision of services to meet customer orders or forecast sales.

Although time periods have been specified here, they should be used only as a guide. Moreover, you will find that those given are at the upper limits for most small businesses. In many instances, particularly for very small businesses, aggregate planning may be no more than for a few months ahead with operations control covering the new few weeks. What distinguishes long-term from aggregate planning is that the latter is made on the basic assumption that the addition of new facilities is excluded as a capacity option for consideration within the time horizon under review.

Other factors which will affect the choice of period covered by aggregate planning and operations control will include the growth characteristics of each market segment, and the length of time the product or service takes to go through the process. A business involved in manufacturing a short-cycle product in a stable market will work on planning and control dimensions of something in the order of three months and three weeks respectively. However, a business involved in a long-duration process (for example, six to nine months) and in a growth market will need to control its operations in detail up to some 12 months ahead and be looking to make aggregate planning decisions from 18 months onwards. Just as long-term capacity issues (e.g., plant delivery lead times) will also affect the appropriate time horizon choice, so will the make-to-order or make-to-stock characteristics of the products/services involved.

The rest of this chapter deals firstly with the aggregate planning and then the operations control tasks which face businesses, and explains the bases on which these procedures should be developed.

Aggregate planning

Aggregate plans must work within the **lead time capacity constraints imposed by the long-term plan**. The purpose of the aggregate planning task, therefore, concerns how these resources should best be used.

The term 'aggregate planning' is used because the plan adopted reviews the capacity requirements for the total (i.e., aggregate) of **all products/services**. The procedure evaluates the demand forecast for this intermediate time horizon in order to establish the **overall or aggregate capacity requirement** for these sales. Since the plans are general, the calculations are simplified by grouping together the forecast sales of like products/services and then expressing, the capacity requirements for these groups in total (for example, metres of cable, number of design hours, weeks of consultancy).

The aim of the 'aggregate plan' is to:

1. Ensure that there is **sufficient capacity** to meet the forecasts.
2. Determine the **best plan to meet the forecast demand** – this will

include assessing the trade-offs involved between inventory holding, overtime, additional shifts, rates of throughput, size of the workforce, the ratio between permanent and temporary staff, sub-contracting, and so on.

Five main **analytical tasks** have to be completed in the process of aggregate planning:

1. **sales forecasts** drawn up for each product or service over the appropriate planning period (usually three months, six months, one year or longer – see the earlier comments on time horizons and types of business).
2. Total cumulative demand for these product forecasts made into **one aggregate demand for all the production processes**. This will require capacity to be expressed in one or more homogeneous units of measurement.
3. The aggregate demand for each time period transformed into staff, processes and other elements of **productive capacity**.
4. Alternative resource schemes developed for meeting the **cumulative capacity requirements**.
5. The most appropriate plan which meets **aggregate demand at the lowest operating costs** selected.

A business may take one or two basic approaches here:

1. **A top-down approach**. This takes the **demand forecasts** for a product group and **estimates the capacity requirements** in line with them. This method is, therefore, based on a set of assumptions both within the product groups (the parts) and then the overall total (the whole) which is deduced from the parts. The methods used in top-down approaches to aggregate planning range from those based on judgement (e.g., intuition or trial and error) to those based on modelling alternative costs (for example, the simplex method of linear programming).[1]

2. **A bottom-up approach** (called rough-cut planning). This method uses a **database for each product** and the capacity requirement for the total demand is compiled from this information. The method, therefore, lends itself to evaluating the overall plan, with individual product plans being revised as the procedure for matching alternative capacity/demand configurations. Furthermore, it also allows rough-cut assessments of the capacity requirements (especially for key processes, i.e. those processes where capacity constraints are known to exists) necessary to meet product/volume forecasts.

---

[1] For those interested in developing these approaches, see Gaither,1980; Stevenson, 1982; Schonberger, 1981; and Vollman, Berry and Wybark, 1984.

Requirements within an aggregate plan

If all demand was uniform then planning resource requirements would be relatively simple and straightforward. The problem is that demand is not uniform. One important decision facing most business, therefore, is to select the appropriate **strategy for organizing resources to meet these demand variations**. In principle, there are three options:

1. **Level production**. Output is kept steady by absorbing fluctuations in demand with inventory levels rising and falling, or order backlog shortening or lengthening in line with demand changes, or by actually manipulating demand patterns.
2. **Chase demand**. Throughput rates are linked to demand and hence capacity adjustments are made in line with sales.
3. **Mixed plan**. This approach uses a combination of level production and chase demand to resolve the sales fluctuations anticipated from one period to the next.

To interpret the appropriateness of the options to meet a particular business's requirements a thorough appreciation of the **implications of each option** is required. This is now provided.

LEVEL PRODUCTION

1. **Inventory**. Inventory is a way of absorbing fluctuations in demand by transferring work to a future time period, and so it is possible to make goods or produce services in one time period to be sold in the next (see Figure 6.1). However, this has drawbacks:

- Inventory is costly, and in some businesses may be subject to **obsolescence**.
- Service operations cannot easily hold inventory. These businesses for the most part must therefore either staff for peak levels or **attempt to change their demand patterns**

2. **Order backlog**. This approach to absorbing fluctuations in demand means that your customers will have to wait before their orders are processed, and it may lead to loss of orders if the delay gets 'excessive'. Where this approach is adopted it is most important to ensure that the **delivery promise is met**, and not to chance failure by being too optimistic.

3. **Demand patterns**. The final option is to change the pattern of sales demand **by attracting sales to periods of low demand**. This could be achieved by advertising and other promotional programmes

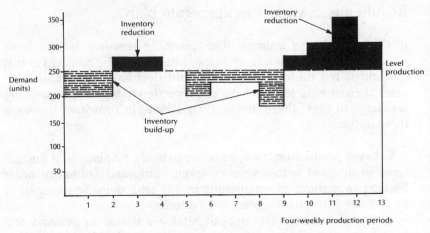

Figure 6.1   Forecast demand over 13 four-week periods met by a combination of level production and inventory build-ups and reductions

(e.g., discounts) together with seeking complementary products/ service such that the high sales of one are at a time of low demand for another (e.g., out-of-season offers at resort hotels). Changing the pattern of demand is particularly useful to most service as well as make-to-order manufacturing businesses. In both of these instances, it is difficult (or even impossible) to prepare or make ahead of demand, and therefore this approach is often the most practical way of smoothing out demand/capacity imbalances. In addition, service businesses may also be able to reshape demand by allocating (where possible) routine activities to the times of low demand. Regular clients are, for example, encouraged to attend on certain days or periods of each day. This leaves the non-routine demand peaks to coincide more with what would then be the times of 'more available' capacity.

CHASE DEMAND

1. **Overtime**. Working overtime hours is a common way of meeting changes in demand. However, not only does this incur premium payments (i.e., the increase over basic rate such as the 'half' in 'time and a half') but periods of overtime can also lead to employees relying on this enhanced level of gross pay and tending to pace themselves over the longer working week. In addition, it reduces the available time in which the necessary **maintenance work** can be carried out without interrupting throughput.

2. **Sub-contract**. The basic make or buy decision concerned the

question of which parts of the process would be completed outside and which were to be completed internally. However, a business may also decide to sub-contract work for which it has the **capability but not the capacity** due to an overall increase in (or the fluctuating nature of) sales demand. This decision will increase the costs of the work involved and also potentially offer **less control over quality and delivery**. In many situations – often when your business is in a period of high sales – then overall market sales will also be high. As a consequence, sub-contract capacity may be difficult to find (or at best orders will be taken under pressure).

3. **Varying the workforce**. A business may take on temporary labour for a period in order to meet an increase in demand. Such a plan, incurs the **employment costs** of advertising, recruitment, shift premiums where applicable, training costs and the inefficiencies which go hand-in-hand with temporary personnel. In addition, unless these increases in capacity are met by an additional shift, then a business would need to have adequate **process investment** for the peak workforce level.

MIXED PLAN

A business may decide to meet sales demand changes by using a combination of the previous two alternatives. In this way, it is able to select **that strategy or combination of strategies which suits it best**.

To illustrate these alternatives Figures 6.1–6.3 are provided, which represent the forecast sales of a small business making a range of

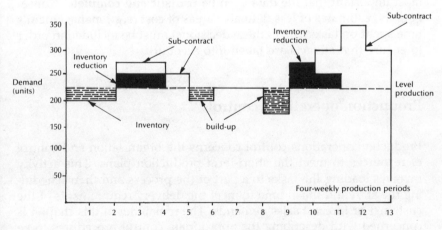

Figure 6.2   Mixed plan using level production with both inventory and sub-contract decisions to meet demand fluctuations

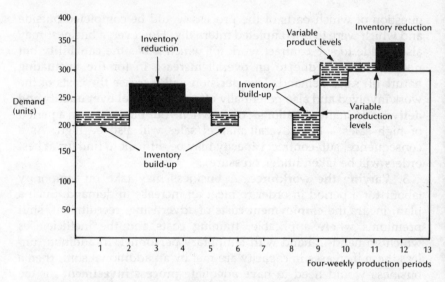

Figure 6.3   Mixed plan using both inventory build-ups and reductions with variable production levels achieved by increasing the workforce in Periods 9–13

bedroom and dining room furniture of a simple design and to standard construction. The sales were assessed in terms of the number of standard units, where a standard unit equated to an amount of capacity throughout the manufacturing processes involved. Each of these three figures represents an alternative aggregate plan to meet these needs. The next step to be undertaken by the company was to evaluate each plan in cost terms and then select that plan which proved to be the most cost-effective. In this assessment, however, it is most important that the data used be **realistic and complete**. Consequently, estimates of less definable areas of cost (e.g., management's time spent on tasks due to these decisions) must be included in order to ensure that all facts are taken into account.

Production/operations control

Production/operations control concerns the organisation and control of resources to meet the short-term production plans. This activity involves loading the tasks to a part of the process and then scheduling the start and finish time to meet the delivery requirements of the customer or forecast sales demands. The remainder of this chapter is concerned with describing the appropriate control procedures to be used against the process choice described in Chapter 2:

1. **Project process**, which is chosen only when a business is engaged in selling and constructing unique, large-scale products/services.
2. **Jobbing process**, for the provision of one-off products/services to meet a requirement specified by a particular customer.
3. **Batch process**, the most common way to organise resources to produce goods or services.
4. **Line process**, where the production tasks are organised as a continuous sequence of events.

Project

The project process is chosen by a business engaged in selling unique, often large-scale products/services. To control this type of activity **network analysis** is used. In addition, networks are very useful in setting up a new business which is itself, of course, a unique task. For this reason it is dealt with in some detail.

NETWORK ANALYSIS AS A CONTROL ACTIVITY

1. **Symbols used**. Three symbols are used in building up a network (see Figure 6.4).

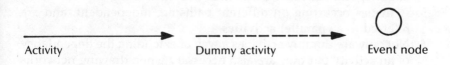

Activity   Dummy activity   Event node

Figure 6.4   Symbols used to draw materials

(a) **Activities** are tasks which have a time duration.
(b) **Events**, on the other hand, signal that an activity is (or number of activities are)finished, and that other activities depending upon them finishing are now able to start.
(c) **Dummy activities** are used as a way of extending the dependency of an activity, and will be explained more fully below.

2. **Building the network**. There are three steps involved in building a network; each is now considered in detail.

(a) **Plan**. Establish all the **activities or steps** involved to complete the task, the time they take, which activities are to be com-

pleted before hand, (known as dependent activities), and draw
the network.

(b) **Schedule**. Apply any **limiting factors** to the network – for
example, time, costs and the availability of people, processes
and materials.

(c) **Control**. Use the network as an **ongoing control by obtaining
feedback** on what has or is happening and **modifying the plan**
in the light of these changes.

1. PLAN

Listing all the activities involved in a task provides not only essential
data for the network but also a worthwhile business discipline. Those
activities which **depend upon other activities being accomplished
before they can start** must also be established.

When this stage has been completed, the network may be drawn.
Figures 6.7, 6.8 and 6.9 illustrate what networks will look like, but a
few guidelines on the DO's and DON'Ts may first prove useful.

1. Activities **start and end with an event**.
2. Any number of activities can **go into or come out of an event**.
3. Where possible, **activities should be drawn from left to right**.
4. Activities occurring on the same path are dependent upon one
   another, and are called **sequential activities**.
5. Activities occurring on different paths are independent, and are
   referred to as **parallel activities**.
6. Not only are dummy activities a way of extending the dependency
   of an activity but they are also necessary when drawing networks
   (see Figure 6.5). In this example, which is part of a larger network,
   Activity Q cannot start until Activities N and P have been completed. Although both segments of the alternative networks express this, only version (2) is correct. (Figure 6.5 illustrates several
   of these guidelines, and serves as a useful entry to the short-
   exercise that follows.)

Now consider the list of activities and their dependencies shown in
Figure 6.6. The network to express this is given in Figure 6.7, but
have a go yourself before checking the solution. Note that networks
always begin with that activity (or those activities) which **do not
depend upon any other activities before they can start**.

2. SCHEDULE

As a means of controlling one-off tasks, a network not only represents the activities and their dependencies in diagramatic form, but

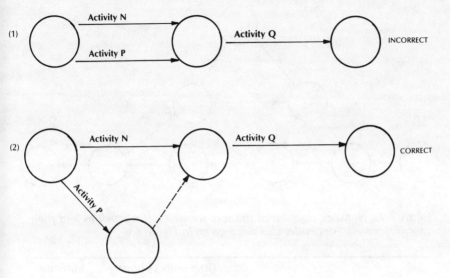

Figure 6.5 Introducing the use of a dummy activity

Activity	Activities on which it is dependent
A	B and C
B	E
C	E
D	–
E	D
F	D
G	E and F
H	G
J	A and H

Figure 6.6 Activities and their dependencies to complete a given task

is also based on **time**. The next step in the procedure, therefore, is to put time against each activity and then, with some simple calculations, use this information both as a control mechanism and a way of identifying those tasks on which to concentrate your efforts. Figure 6.7 lists the activities involved by a small business engaged in removing old windows and installing new, Georgian-style ones in their place. Although occasionally more than one window would be installed at a site, an analysis revealed that a little over 75 per cent of all jobs involved a single window installation.

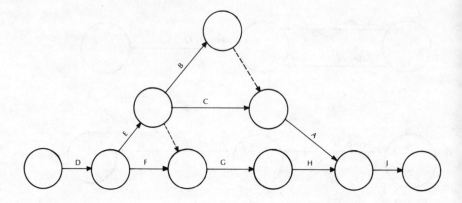

Figure 6.7   Network diagram of the task for which the activities and their dependencies were given in Figure 6.6

| Activity | Time units ($\frac{1}{2}$ hour) to do the task, depending on the number of men (1, 2, or 3) available | | | Minimum number of men required to do the job |
	1	2	3	
Load vehicle at yard and prepare	2	1	1	1
To site	2	2	2	1
Unload and check the window size	$\frac{1}{2}$	1	$\frac{1}{2}$	1
Prepare site	2	$1\frac{1}{2}$	1	1
Remove old window frame	$1\frac{1}{2}$	$1\frac{1}{2}$	1	1
Offer new window to the opening	–	1	1	2
Load old window frame to vehicle	1	$\frac{1}{2}$	–	1
Finish installation	4	3	2	1
Load tools, etc. to vehicle	1	$\frac{1}{2}$	–	1
Return to yard	2	2	2	1
Load old frame and tools to vehicle	2	1	$\frac{1}{2}$	

Table 6.1   Activities involved and other details to take out an old window and instal a new, premeasured one on site

The network to represent these activities and their dependencies is given as Figure 6.8. Sales for this small business began to increase and there were days when it became necessary to instal a new window on two sites on the same day. However, as is common at times of sales growth, the company wished to keep capital investment to a minimum (for this company, it concerned avoiding the purchase of a second vehicle) as well as wanting to keep labour costs to a minimum. Using the information given in Table 6.1, Figure 6.9 shows the use of networks as a way of representing how this could be done. To arrive

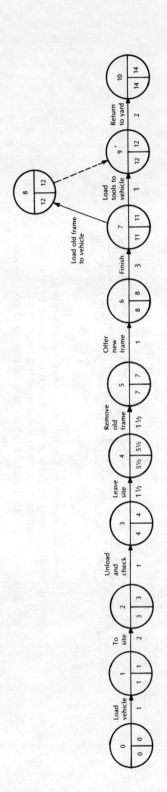

Figure 6.8 Network diagram of the data in Table 6.1

120

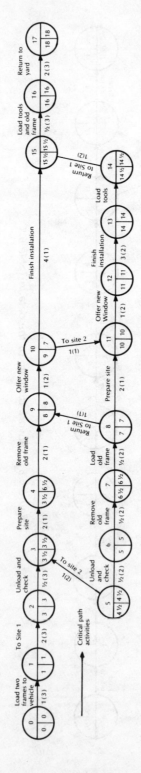

Figures in brackets indice the number of men involved

Activity 'Load 2 frames to vehicle' with 3 men is the same time as for loading 1 frame to vehicle with 2 men

Activities 'to site 2' and 'Return to site 1' are estimated at one ½-hour unit each

Activity 'Load tools and old frame' between Events 15 and 16 includes both time elements for these two activities

Figure 6.9 Network diagram: instal new window at two separate sites

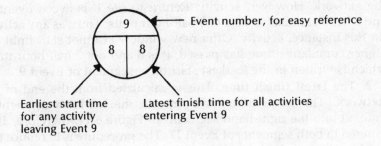

Figure 6.10 Information contained in the event nodes in Figure 6.9

at this solution it was first necessary to put times on to the network, which will be explained below, and also review alternatives. It was from these that the one showing the lowest overall time was chosen.

The revised work procedure selected by the business and illustrated in Figure 6.9 shows that one window could be installed on two different sites using three men and one vehicle. The time taken for this was 18 half-hour units (or nine hours' working time) for each of three men as opposed to seven hours' working (14 half-hour units) for each of four men (i.e., two men on each site). Although the total man hours for the revised method were slightly less, the labour costs (due to overtime premiums) would be about the same. However, for this small business the important gain was that it did not have to invest in a second vehicle, especially at a time when sales growth put a still higher premium on cash resources.

To help control the activities represented by a network and to highlight those activities (or sets of activities) which are critical to completing the job on time (referred to as the **critical path**, and explained later), the earliest start and latest finish times need to be calculated. Figure 6.10 shows the information contained in one of the event nodes in the network shown as Figure 6.9

1. **The earliest start time**. This is calculated from the beginning of the network by **cumulating the time units for all sequential activities**. In Figure 6.9 activity 'Load two frames to vehicle' takes 1 half-hour unit, and this is entered in the left-hand segment of the Event Node 1 as shown. Then, activity 'To site', which takes 2 half-hour units, is added to the left-hand segment of the previous event and the new total of 3 is entered into the left-hand segment of Event Node 2, and so on. Where two or more activities enter the same event, then it is the **higher or highest cumulative total** which is the figure used. For example, 'Remove old frame' between Events 4 and 9 would lead to a cumulative time of 7 half-hour units at that stage of

the network. However, activity 'Return to site 1' between Events 8 and 9 has a cumulative time of 8 half-hour units. Thus, as any activity (in this instance, activity 'Offer new window') cannot start until the higher cumulative time has passed, it is 8 and not 7 half-hour units which is written in the 'earliest start time' segment of Event 9.

2. **The latest finish time**. This is calculated from the end of the network. The same cumulative time in the left-hand segment is entered into the right-hand segment. In Figure 6.11, therefore, 18 is entered in both segments of Event 17. The procedure is to reduce this total by the length of time taken by the preceding activity and enter the remainder into the latest finish time of the appropriate node. In Figure 6.11, activity 'Return to yard' taking 2 half-hour units is subtracted and the remainder (i.e., 16 half-hour units) is entered accordingly. However, where two or more activities back into the same event, then it is the **smaller or smallest 'remainder'** which is used. Activity 'Finish installation' between Events 15 and 10 takes 4 half-hour units. Thus $15.5 - 4 = 11.5$. However, activity 'To site 2' from Event 11 to Event 10 taking 1 half-hour unit brings with it a remainder of 9. Thus, the smaller residue of 9 is the one which is entered. This is because the latest finish time for an activity or activities entering Event 10 (in this instance, activity 'Offer new window') **must be after 9 half-hour units have passed**. If it is later than this then the whole network (i.e., the job) will be delayed accordingly.

3. **The critical path**. This introduces the concept of the critical path. An important aspect of any job is **how long it will take to complete**. The critical path is the set of activities through the network whose cumulative time is the greatest. This represents the earliest the job will be done, and thus delays to any activities on this critical path will also extend the completion time.

It can be seem that those activities where the earliest start and latest finish times **are the same** will form the critical path. There are several ways to mark this, and one such way is shown on Figure 6.11. Where there is a gap between the earliest start and latest finish times then this is referred to as 'slack' and in more complex networks will be part of the information recorded in the event node.

3. CONTROL

A network is the best way to control project-type work. When it is being used as a control, information on **what is actually happening** will be fed back so that it can be updated. On larger networks than those shown in this chapter, the impact of these changes would then be recorded and, where required, a new critical path established.

A final note on using networks for larger projects is the concept of establishing **key dates**. Before the job begins, certain dates throughout the network are formally selected to review progress. Besides providing a reviewing opportunity, this approach is also a way of preventing the slack time in one phase of the project being used up by a later phase. If this were allowed to happen, then the result would be a situation where many sets of activities would become critical and deadlines would invariably have to be extended.

Jobbing

A small business which adopts jobbing as the appropriate operations process will be involved in providing one-off products/services to meet a requirement specified by the customer. The control system, therefore, loads only jobs for which an order has been received. It then needs to ensure that the job goes through the **required sequence of operations** and that the **agreed delivery date is met**.

Because the exact nature of the job may be unsure and its duration uncertain there is a need to provide for this uncertainty in the control procedure. The delivery agreement would have to include an allowance to cover this uncertainty and it will be necessary to establish **revision dates** against which progress can be monitored. As this will also be a make-to-order business then a backlog of orders will start to build up, the extent of which needs to be part of the delivery promise in two ways. First, to allow for the time it will take the order in question to enter the process (and so reflect the new size of the order backlog); second, for the job quotation to specify that the delivery time quoted will be from the receipt of the order.

The control of the jobbing process will itself be in two parts:

1. The need to show the **overall requirement compared to available capacity**.
2. The need to monitor the progress of an order recognising that the detailed hour-by-hour or day-by-day control will be in the hands of the person responsible for completing the job.

A typical way to do this is through a bar chart similar to Figure 6.11. This relatively simple control was adopted by a small business to control the allocation and loading of the consultants it employed. It also provided a means of assessing the progress made on each assignment, the position of each job in terms of days remaining and days of work to be done, and the assigned and potential workload in the future.

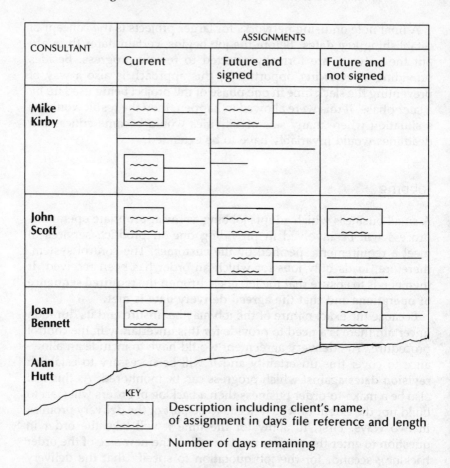

Figure 6.11 Bar chart representing the actual and proposed assignments allocated to management consultants

The bar chart in Figure 6.11 (together with the file details) would provide an overall check on the loading per consultant with the days remaining shown to scale (e.g., 1cm = 1 day), and updated each week. If required, a colour-coded system could be used to illustrate a single or two consultants working arrangement, a part-time or full-time working basis, the length of and any extensions to the original assignment, and days left against the quoted days agreed with the client. In this latter case, a simple way would be to add a different coloured bar to the end of the 'days left' bar to show the extent of the overrun. Each assignment would be moved from the right to the left as its category changed, and in this way discussions with clients on general and specific availability would embrace the **actual and potential overall commitments of the business**.

Batch

When a business selects a batch process it will reflect the change in its sales from one-off, low volume to repeat, higher-volume products/ services. Because in batch a job is broken down into a series of operations, the order quantities issued will be for a number of products/services, and by definition these will also be competing for common processes. As a consequence the control task will involve monitoring jobs through the process and also assessing the impact of the **volume and product/service mix changes over time** against specific process capacities, and particularly the known **key processes** (i.e., those processes where **capacity constraints are known to exist**).

A typical control procedure used is to break down each order into the sequence of operations involved and then, having assessed the time required to do each operation, load each job into the process. At the same time, it will be necessary to ensure that the total loading for each process does not exceed the available capacity. Where it does, then the loading programme will have to be adjusted, as mentioned when discussing the 'rough-cut' approach at the aggregate planning stage. This latter exercise needs detailed implementation for **key processes** (i.e. bottlenecks), whereas with many other processes capacity will always be well in excess of overall requirement. In order to cope with the large amount of information involved, a microcomputer will often be the only sensible way to handle this control task. As the use of microprocessors is suitable for both production/ operations control, as well as inventory control a note explaining their use and some general points to bear in mind when considering them is provided in the Appendix at the end of this chapter. In addition, some points about their specific application to production control are given on pp. 129–37.

Whether using a manual or microprocessor-based system, the control principles will be similar. As explained earlier, the basis for loading jobs on to the process is to break each one into the operations specified on the planning sheet. This information, provided as one of the premanufacturing process documents, will include:

- Code numbers.
- Drawing numbers.
- Material specifications.
- Component descriptions.
- Operation descriptions.
- Process on which each operation is to be completed.
- Tooling details.
- Set-up times and process times involved for each of the operations.
- Order quantity sizes to be issued.

From this 'master' information, a route card will be produced for the particular order quantity to be manufactured which will give the planning sheet information (and normally, additional columns to record the quantities made or rejected, inspection details, planned date requirements at each operation and actual completion dates). One well-used paperwork system provides a booklet of cards, one for each operation, together with a master sheet. This allows for the return of each completed operation card as a feedback to the central control function, with the balance of the booklet, a copy of the planning sheet, relevant copies of drawings and so on remaining with the job throughout. In this way the progress of the job through the manufacturing processes can be monitored against the plan, and decisions concerning 'higher than planned for' scrap and behind-schedule work can be made at the earliest opportunity.

Particularly in batch manufacturing processes, it is important to be aware of certain essential details required to improve the accuracy of loading in order to ensure that the plan is realistic, process capacity is not overloaded, and delivery promises can be met. This includes:

1. The **accuracy of set-up and process times**.
2. **Queueing times** involved while other jobs are being completed.
3. **Tool wear** and the effect on process times and scrap levels.
4. **Material variation**, and the effects on process times.
5. **Varying operator skill levels** and the impact on the practical task of allocating jobs.
6. **Actual plant efficiency and breakdowns** leading to realistic statements of capacity.

It is important to ensure that the planning of jobs through the required information processes takes into account the fact that the production control system will often need to reroute jobs due to **capacity bottlenecks**. It is therefore a sound policy to supply both preferred and alternative routings at the planning stage and then for these to be reflected in the costing system. In this way planning flexibility is provided without the disadvantages of incurring the cost of excesses when using an alternative routing.

If your business is involved in making products which are simple to manufacture or the content of the non-standard items is high in proportion to the standard, it may often be adequate to apply a much less involved approach to the loading task by using certain rules of thumb, for instance:

1. Stating that so many operations can be completed in a **given period of time** (e.g., a day or a week).
2. Working backwards from the delivery date and, using this general

rule, calculate the **start date** in order to complete the job on time.

At the lower end of the small business spectrum, however, it is doubtful if any form of loading should be adopted. This is because the size of the overall task is much smaller and delivery and bottleneck problems can be overcome by the greater flexibility inherent in both process and labour capacity. If a control is adopted, then it should be very simple otherwise the costs of control will outweigh the improvements in efficiency. What normally happens is that scheduling difficulties are overcome by manual intervention or quickly arranged overtime working. By thinking ahead and discussing workloads and availability with those concerned, scheduling changes can be recognised and discussed and agreement reached which suits the customer, your workforce and yourself.

Line

Because of the high volumes on which the choice of line process is based, the operations required to manufacture a product are laid out in the line. The control problems are therefore concerned with keeping a line fed with the components and sub-assemblies required to meet the programme. Materials requirement planning (MRP) is the basis of the control system used here. An MRP system essentially takes the sales forecasts for each item and then calculates the sub-assemblies and components necessary to make these anticipated product requirements. In this way, it establishes a **component and sub-assembly programme** to feed the assembly programme in the next or later in the same production period (see also Chapter 7).

Because the component and sub-assembly volumes (i.e., quantity × work content) are much smaller, these requirements will normally be met by batch processes and controlled accordingly.

Microprocessors and production/operations control

Although similar production/operations control principles will be used for either a manually-operated system, one backed by some form of data processing or a combination of both, it would be quite wrong to suppose that it is possible to take an existing clerical procedure and adapt it directly for computer operation.

This is because many clerical systems depend upon **one or several individuals' job knowledge and intervention** to make them work

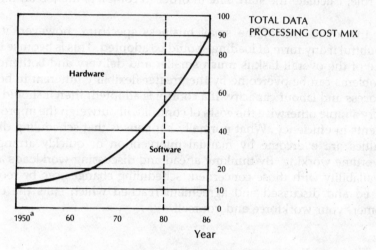

a In 1950, hardware represented 90 per cent of total cost;
in 1985 it represented about 30 per cent
Source: Friedrichs and Schaff (1983)

Figure 6.12   Data processing costs

effectively, and knowledge which has been collected over the years
and invariably not recorded or passed on to others. Yet it is this same
information and working knowledge which is critical to the effective
working of a production/operations control system, no matter whether
it is clerically-or data processing-based.

Although many applications for microprocessors are justified by
their cost savings, often the greater benefits which accrue from using
them to control production/operations come from reductions in
inventory, the greater profits that accrue from the increase in volume
that can be provided from the same resources, and improvements in
meeting deliveries.

Partly because the development (and subsequent price reductions)
of the hardware has been so rapid, and partly because the creation of
software is so labour intensive that there is a shortage of software
worldwide, a change in the total data processing cost mix has taken
place, as shown in Figure 6.12. However, it is most important to
realise that the pressure to reduce software costs has to be resisted if
this results in a system which **does not meet the needs of the control
problem**.

Conclusion

The effective control of the production/operations function in a business is an essential prerequisite for profit and growth. However, many small businesses neither recognise the incremental way in which the complexity of control problems increase with a growth in sales or a widening of the product/service range provided, nor the fact that it is more difficult to argue for investment in control improvements and to support these proposals by tangible cost savings. However, the improvements which result from sound planning and control developments are both real and substantial. Recent research[1] revealed that for the 30 per cent of small business who modernised their production function in the early 1980s, the investment breakdown was:

Investment category	Total (%)
Plant modernisation	75
Building improvement	20
Introduction of computers	5

Of the small businesses who had modernised their administrative (37 per cent) and their selling (33 per cent) functions, 62 per cent and 15 per cent respectively had achieved this with the introduction of computers. Although this is far from being conclusive, it does tend to support the view that computers are often introduced into small businesses on the basis of 'cost saving achieved' arguments, rather than for the less tangible advantages associated with delivery performance and capacity utilisation improvements. It is most important, if this is so, for small businesses to recognise (and then assess) the extent of these less-tangible gains so fundamental to overall business performance and success, but which can so easily be overlooked.

Appendix: Choosing and using a computer

Investing in computers can result in a business acquiring anything between an expensive, under-used piece of equipment to a significant aid for improv-

---

[1] These results are taken from Mendham, 1983. Of the small businesses completing the questionnaire, 58 per cent claimed they had modernised their businesses over the last two years, and the 30 per cent quoted above related to this 58 per cent.

ing its overall performance. The computer can become a time-consuming distraction or a time-saving tool. It represents an investment in time and money which requires **careful analysis and thoughtful management**. Having said this, however, there is no question about the trends. The most competitive companies (including those in the small business sector) are increasingly the ones employing appropriate business tools for dealing with different tasks. Where these are repetitive clerical tasks, repetitive analytical tasks, repetitive reporting and information searches and repetitive production/operations control tasks, then computers are likely to figure in their solution.

A key issue for the small business when considering investing in computers is the degree of **data repetition which must be handled**. In a competitive environment, the speed of response to meet requirements or providing service information needs is increasingly vital to winning and retaining orders – but this has to be balanced by the costs associated with any apparent improvements brought about by computer technology. In addition, it is most important to recognise that purchasing computer hardware is only one of a number of equally critical tasks when 'choosing and using a computer'. There are many pitfalls in the decision to 'computerise', including the wrong:

- **Tasks** identified for computerisation.
- Computer **system** chosen.
- **Software (programs)** purchased.
- **People** using the computer.
- Type of **training** provided.

The list could easily be extended to include many other areas of potential mistakes. However, failure to update a business's techniques to help manage and control can be equally costly. Computers are not only here to stay but they will play a greater role in personal, commercial and business life over the next decade. In the home, television sets are already linked to data computers (for example, Teletext and Oracle) and consumers can now do their shopping through this medium. In large organisations, the 'electronic office' is becoming a reality and this development should not be ignored by small companies. Offices which use only typewriters and which ignore the value of word processors may well be losing out in the drive for overall productivity.

Is a computer required?

There is obviously a need to carry out a careful assessment before deciding on whether or not to purchase a computer. The starting point is usually to define the 'symptoms' which suggest that a computer might be helpful. Typical symptoms include:

- **Invoices** taking too long to process.
- Not knowing readily **who owes you money**.
- **Monthly accounts delayed**, and less useful as a consequence.
- The accounting function becoming complex and slow to respond to the business needs. This in turn is affecting the **monetary controls, cash flows, or supplier and customer service**.
- Increased business volumes putting **existing manual systems under pressure**.
- The back-up service to customers deteriorating. For example, **inventory**

levels are unclear and delivery date control is becoming a problem.
- The existing **payroll system** – manual, slow and not dependable.
- **Repetitive typing of information** – a poor image, wasted resources and prone to error.
- Clerical and administrative support, though high, proving **inadequate**.

There are, however, some reasons which are **not valid**:

- The need to **reduce staff levels**.
- Using a computer to improve an **underdeveloped manual system** which needs updating.
- 'Computers are becoming popular, so we should have one'.

These are not valid because it is most important to distinguish between those gains which will come from improving a less than effective system and those which come from the proposed alternative. The first two points above can equally be gained by introducing improvements to existing manual systems whilst the third is (at best) a guess that improvements will come from this investment and (at worst) window-dressing and a poor use of scarce resources.

What can computers do?

If there is initial evidence to suggest that there really is a need for a computer, then devote enough time to understanding more fully the various, possible functions which may be of use to you. Talk to a local retail shop by all means, but recognise that their job is to sell the hardware rather than advise on selection. There is usually a need to talk to more specialised agents or even to invest time in talking to a consultant. But, also be prepared to **learn and understand** the basic business issues involved – reading one or more of the popular computer journals is a start.[1] Beware of statements that computers can 'do anything'. There are also the dangers of choosing a system which is limited and inflexible or choosing one which is too complex. The penalty for 'getting it wrong' can be measured in both terms of **costs** (£) and the **time** involved. The first step is to recognise that **computers perform three basic groups of tasks**:

1. **Storage and quick access to data**.
2. The facility to **analyse (or manipulate) data**.
3. The basis for **control and/or monitoring systems**.

1. **Storage and quick access to data** involves a group of tasks including personnel records, payroll provision, service counter, stock records and information, purchasing records, debtors, creditors, price lists, parts list and word processing!
   The larger and more complex the business becomes then the wider the range of data which needs to be handled. Two warnings need to be heeded, however:

- To be able to put data on to a computer, then **good, manual systems must already exist**.

---

[1] For example, *Personal Computer World, Practical Computing, Which Computer?*; also trade journals such as *Business Weekly*.

- Putting the information into a computer (i.e., **creating a database**) is in itself a time-consuming task; it may require quite a lot of work to convert an existing manual system to one suitable to be handled by a computer system – the choice of appropriate 'software' is important and the tendency to underestimate the time involved must be avoided.
- Careful attention must be paid to ensuring **integrity and security of the data** for often a long time period (years); the software as well as the hardware needs **maintenance**, this all costs money.

The exception is where the computer is used exclusively as a wordprocesssor, and in this case the 'database' can be purchased in an immediately usable form.

Using a computer as a wordprocessor or purchasing a dedicated wordprocessing machine can be a difficult decision. Current prices range widely, depending on function/performance choice. Three key criteria, however, can aid the choice of wordprocessors:

- Quality of **letter reproduction** (e.g., print quality and layout).
- **Speed of production**.
- Degree of **repetition or variety to be handled**.

2. **The facility to analyse (or manipulate) data** involves carrying out routine analysis and producing some form of report or statement of refined data. This can substantially improve the performance of a business whether it is a regular or routine activity. However, great care needs to be exercised in choosing the task (**i.e., the type of analysis**) to be computerised, the right computer hardware and finally the appropriate program or software package. Each decision point is critical. The typical, analytical questions to which a computer might be asked to provide answers would include the sales over the last month, profit levels this year, output or delivery performance, shortfalls in output or expected profit levels 'if sales increased by £x and prices decreased by £y'. All are examples of repetitive analysis, require a database to be created and, therefore, imply some of the problems outlined above.

3. **Basis for control and/or monitoring system** – creating this involves a higher level of complexity and, as implied, needs a greater time and cash investment. Control systems range from the simple 'one task' systems to sophisticated multitask production scheduling and machine control systems. Any related and dependent series of events can be linked in a computerised control system, but the more costly the system becomes the greater the computing power required. Examples include the control of component flow, shopfloor machine loading, automatic reordering for service stocks and process control.

Choosing the most suitable machine/system

There are three basic levels of 'computing power' which can be purchased:

Computer type	Price range (£)	Level of power
Micro	90–10,000	Lower
Mini	7,000–50,000	↓
Mainframe	100,000–10 million	Higher

The microcomputer will meet most needs of the majority of departments and small businesses. Beyond this, the investment costs involved will require a totally different cost–benefit review. Advice on minicomputers is an expert's job. A small business would, however, never need to purchase a mainframe which are generally owned and run by 'computer bureaux' which will readily provide advice on the range of services available.

Choosing a microcomputer

Choosing a microcomputer is potentially difficult as there are currently well over 100 machine types. They can be separated into four broad categories:

- Games machines with **limited data processing capability**.
- Wordprocessors as a **dedicated or multifunctional facility**.
- Micros for **completing data (record) processing and data analyses**.
- Micros for **control purposes**.

The 'size' and 'complexity' of the task determines the choice. The key to this decision is in writing down the specification of the tasks in some detail – there is no short cut! One useful check list of issues to be covered in customising a specification is given below:[1]

- A brief description of the **business, its location, products and plans**. Then answer the following questions:
- 'Why do you want to computerise?'
- 'What do you want to computerise' (i.e., an outline of the applications)?
- The **data types, volumes and response times** involved.
- The level of **expansion capability** required – so often the business out-grows a computer after a couple of years
- In what way do **your requirements appear to be unique**?

In arriving at the specification, it is useful to bear in mind the three phases of work which a computer carries out, and to assess the tasks to be computerised and the mix of these in volume in the work to be undertaken. These

[1] Extract from a paper produced by Kidsons (Consultants), Bank House, 8 Cherry Street, Birmingham B2 5AD.

phases are:

- **Typing in** the data.
- **Processing** the results.
- **Printing and/or displaying** the results, instructions or text.

Identifying the mix facilitates the hardware selection by helping to identify the hardware characteristics with those of the applications to be made. Making an estimate of the time required for each phase will help in assessing the shape of the activities involved in its use. In addition, it is necessary to estimate:

- The **memory size of the micro required**.
- The **disc capacity of the micro** – note that there are two main types of disc:

1. Floppy discs which tend to be cheap, relatively slow and currently cannot hold more than 1 million characters of data. These drives are now available in a 'rigid' form.
2. Fixed discs, also known as Winchester Discs: these are expensive, very fast and can hold up to 40 million characters of data.

Decisions on disc capacity need to be taken in parallel with memory provision. It is, however, most advisable to always have two discs per application for reasons of security backup.

The specification then becomes the basis for talking to a range of potential suppliers. Select several and ask each to give you a quotation in writing, setting out the machine choice (or options) and its functions against your specification, price, support costs, degree of compatibility with other machines, and any issues they feel you might have missed.

The process of comparing these replies will give you more information. Further checks include choosing a machine which is still likely to be on the market in two years' time and ensuring that if you need more than one machine for different purposes, they are compatible. Furthermore, if you feel that the system may grow in size or complexity in any significant way it is important to check that the machine has the capacity to cope, for recreating your database in a year's time for a different machine is both very expensive and very time-consuming.

Finally, it is essential to purchase a machine for which programs (software) are readily available.

Using the microcomputer – its software

The purchase of a microcomputer is only the initial step – it provides the 'potential' for taking on a range of specific tasks. To turn it into a 'workhorse' it needs either programming for the specific requirement[1] or the purchase of a ready-made program(s) (i.e., software) to meet the task in hand. This normally comes in the form of a 'floppy' or fixed disc as described earlier, or tapes.

Writing programs for specific applications is not usually necessary and is extremely expensive. Although there is a huge amount of off-the-shelf

---

[1] Hulse, 1980.

software available much of it is designed to be used on specific machines and it is generally best to assume that it is not transferable from one machine to another. The four primary types of programmes for micros are:

- **Demonstration/training packages**, including games.
- **Word processing packages**.
- **Calculation packages** – e.g., VISICALC and other specialist spreadsheets.
- **Database packages**.

The extract below is from the Department of Industry booklet 'Microprocessors and the Small Business'[1] and gives an indication of the wide range of programs available. Advice needs to be sought to ensure that machine, program and applications are all compatible.

List of software packages suitable for office application

- Payroll
- Sales ledger
- Purchase ledger
- General ledger
- Incomplete records accounting
- Direct bank credit
- Bank cheque reconciliation
- VAT calculation
- Tax calculation
- Accounts payable
- Accounts receivable
- Cash control
- Financial planning
- Fixed assets and depreciation
- Investment portfolio
- Lease, rental and hire purchase control
- Lease administration
- Sales analysis
- Budget and cost analysis
- Customer service analysis
- Market survey analysis
- Maintenance scheduling
- Order entry and invoicing
- Word processing
- Mailing lists
- Appointments file
- Personnel files
- Shareholder records
- Graphics
- Statistics
- Production control
- Time/cost recording for employees
- Job costing
- Energy management

---

[1] Hulse, 1980.

When searching out ready-made programs it is important to resist the temptation to select those which offer an extensive set of options, some or many of which may never be needed. The rationale underpinning this is that it will reduce the likelihood of outgrowing the facilities. However, there are important disadvantages which need to be recognised and measured:

1. More complicated software requires a **larger computer to run it**.
2. It will **cost more**.
3. The user will need longer **to learn how to use the program efficiently**.
4. It will involve computer time in **servicing unused option pathways**.
5. **Data entry will probably be slower**.

Keeping this in mind, it is important to search out those programs which meet the detailed requirements of the application. Any other options will become a handicap rather than a benefit. Where program choice is available in terms of the detailed requirements of the application it is essential to seek out the one which is right for **your business and your way of working within it**. Points to consider include:

1. **User-friendliness** – often this requires the operator (and preferably others in the business who will wish to use it) to try the software before purchase.
2. **The reputation of the producer** – as some 25 per cent of software houses go into liquidation each year there is a clear advantage in purchasing programs from a reputable, well-established company. In this way, the opportunity to clarify misunderstandings and anomalies is provided.
3. **Compatibility** – carefully check a vendor's marketing claims that the software is compatible with different hardwares. In many instances programs are, in fact, not 100 per cent compatible, and the position may have further deteriorated due to hardware development since the software was written.
4. **Supporting documentation** – assess the standard of documentation to support a program, in terms of both clarity and thoroughness.
5. **Avoid large-scale changes** – it is important to delete from the preferred list of software options those programs which will necessitate large-scale changes to current working practices. If major system development is required then this should be completed prior to computerisation, even though this may have been the stimulus for action. **Improve the procedure** before investing in programs, training and database provision.

Using these points will reduce the options list to a few. Selections then should be based primarily on the **hardware on which it will be used**.

Implementation

The decision to computerise is potentially complex and expensive but represents an area of 'performance improvement' which cannot be ignored. Most managers should become computer literate over the next few years and

---

[1] Hulse, 1980.

should regularly read one of the popular computer magazines from news-agents and in which the issues and developments are superficially covered. The bibliography provides additional information for choosing and using computers, and for training in their use.

If you intend to introduce a computerised system of any substance it is necessary properly to **plan a programme of the tasks involved** similar to that below;[1]

1. **Implementation plan** – A timetable showing all the events and taking account of the availability of hardware, software and staff capability.
2. **Office Organisation** – Jobs will change. You must consider what and how jobs will be affected, what new procedures will be required and the mix of jobs involved.
3. **Training** – Training must be provided, for all who will come into contact with the computer system or its outputs (**including managers**).
4. **Security** – You need to protect your data against loss and so security procedures need to be planned. You also need a contingency plan to guard against major mishaps.
5. **Testing** – You need to ensure that the computer system is actually producing all you expect of it before you discontinue the old systems.

COSTS IN ADDITION TO THE COMPUTER HARDWARE AND SOFTWARE

There will be costs involved in addition to computer hardware and software:

1. **Computer installation** – You will probably need help in wiring connections, organising discs and several pieces of ancillary equipment.
2. **System set-up** – You need to decide how to construct the 'database'. There is usually a heavy input of data when setting up a system.
3. **Consumables** – Including a supply of continuous stationery, printer, ribbons, daisy wheels, and so on.
4. **Maintenance** – A maintenance contract is advisable to cover both the computer (the hardware) and the software.
5. **Insurance** – The loss of the computer and software should also be covered by an insurance policy.

CHAPTER 7

The Functions of Inventory and its Control in Production/Operations

Introduction

The way in which funds are used in a small business – as indeed in any company – is of paramount importance to its continued prosperity. Table 7.1 gives extracts from the 1982 balance sheets of seven small UK businesses from various manufacturing sectors. It revealed that for most of these companies, inventory was a significant balance sheet entry, averaging overall some 22 per cent of total assets. Furthermore, in five instances, it was considerably larger than the balance sheet entry for plant and equipment, standing an average 1.4 times higher.

The control of inventory, although important to a business, is rarely given adequate attention. Whilst decisions to use funds for plant and equipment, for instance, are normally carefully monitored, the relative effort in controlling inventory is (by and large) too little,

Table 7.1 Balance sheet extracts, seven UK small businesses, £000

Company	Total assets	Plant and equipment (less depre-ciation)	Inventory	Inventory & total assets	Ratio of inventory to plant
Tufnol	3301	393	969	29	2.5
Bar Productions	2253	356	515	23	1.5
Sandalin International	1367	84	168	12	2.0
Copeland and Jenkins	1351	405	184	14	0.5
Hayes, Ford and Eliot	1054	161	236	22	1.5
Birmingham Plastics	702	248	139	20	2.5
Engineering and Glassfibre Developments	416	30	89	21	3.0

Source: Financial accounts of the companies listed

and too late. Increases in inventory occur. The concern and action to reduce and control this significant asset is often made only after the event – the classic 'stable door and horse bolted' syndrome. In this chapter, the types of inventory, their functions, and the practical ways of controlling *them* are explained and the key features embodied in these control tasks highlighted.

Traditional view of inventory

In most businesses inventory is looked upon (and controlled) almost exclusively from the point of view of how it is recorded in the balance sheet. This view is based on defining **where the inventory is found** within the business, rather than **for what it is used**. This view does, however, have a degree of validity because the point at which inventory is found can be defined against three broad areas:

- At the point just prior to the production/operations process, known as **raw material and component inventory**.
- That which occurs during the process of production/operations, called **work-in-progress inventory**.
- As an output from the production/operations process but before it is delivered to the customer, which constitutes **finished goods inventory**.

Inventory which is held at these three points in the total operations process serves quite different purposes within the business; these are briefly illustrated below:

1. **Raw materials and components**. A stockholding of raw materials and components helps a business to:

- Cater for the **variability of supply**.
- Take advantage of **quantity discounts**.
- Provide a cushion against **anticipated price rises**.

2. **Work-in-progress**. Providing work-in-progress inventory allows the production/operations function the opportunity to decouple the processes involved in making a product or providing a service. In this way it facilitates the independence of each operation. If one machine is working on a quantity of products, the next machine need not wait for these to be completed as it is able to draw from a number of jobs held as work-in-progress. Similarly, orders for goods or services are processed at one stage, allocated appropriately and then completed without any stage being dependent on the step before. This leads to:

- Greater **flexibility in scheduling**.
- Improved **utilisation of processes and labour**.
- A levelling out of **different output rates** in each part of the total process.

3. **Finished goods**. In make-to-stock businesses, the opportunity to make for finished goods inventory at this stage offers several advantages by:

- Providing **off-the-shelf customer service**.
- Enabling a company to cope more easily with demand variations by allowing **steady production to be maintained** over a period of time.
- Offering **insurance** against plant breakdown or uncertainty in the supply of materials/components.

The control of inventory

Businesses invest in inventory in order to obtain a mix of the benefits just described. The object in controlling this sizeable asset is, therefore, that of getting value for money. To help assess these trade-offs, information on the amount of inventory held against each function provided is a necessary prerequisite. However, there are two general characteristics about inventory which illustrate, above all, the level of business indifference to its control and the underlying perspective on which the current controls typically used are built.

Firstly, many businesses complete stocktakes on as few occasions as possible; normally they are arranged to coincide with the half-year and year-end accounts. Secondly, the designated categories of inventory are raw materials/components, work-in-progress and finished goods.[1] This choice, however, is made to facilitate the evaluation of inventory as appropriate inputs into the profit and loss account and the balance sheet. The outcome is, therefore, viewed as a provision of information to the accounts function, and not as an opportunity to **create data which will provide important insights into the control of this large asset**.

In contrast, review the detailed analyses which have been developed to help in the capital investment appraisal approaches currently used by accountants. In the seven companies analysed in Table 7.1, inventory stood an average 1.4 times higher than the size of the net plant and machinery, and this is by no means unusual. Businesses thus need to follow the simple maxim of allocating control resources on a pro rata basis – **the bigger the asset, the more it warrants attention**.

Aspects of control

A business holds inventory for a number of reasons. It is therefore most important that it is not grouped into just a few categories which fail to distinguish between the various reasons for holding it. To avoid this, it is necessary to develop a number of categories which characterise a business, and hence provide an insight into **why the inventory is being held**, which gives the key to its **control**. Many businesses treat inventory as being, by and large, the consequence of productions/operations needs and hold the POM function accountable for its control and ultimate reduction. But this is a far too insensitive control device for such a sizeable asset. How can any business justify controlling over 20 per cent of its total assets in this way?

Furthermore, when the date for stocktaking approaches, it is common practice to reduce inventory by holding off purchases at the front end. Also by using different rules in the business, an unrepresentative picture of the pattern of inventory inside the business

---

[1] Statement of Standard Accounting Practice (SSAP) 9, 'Stocks and Work-in-progress', requires that inventory be split into these three categories.

itself can be created – for example, issuing materials prematurely or rushing items inefficiently to the next stage in the process. The rationale for this is that it reduces the clerical burden of stocktaking, which further illustrates the business's view of this datacollecting opportunity. Stocktaking is seen as a chore; it needs to be done in order to meet the legal requirements of the business. This attitude, however, means that a **fundamental control opportunity is lost**.

Categories of inventory

When stocktaking is completed, two distinct yet complementary objectives should have been met. The first is the **evaluation of the amount of inventory in the business**. The second is to provide an answer to the question as to **why it is there**. Inventory should no longer be evaluated by the present, three, common, balance sheet categories but should be broken down into a whole series of categories to provide the basis for better control. Two main categories will in practice be necessary, each with many sub-categories:

1. Corporate inventory.
2. Production/operations inventory.

CORPORATE INVENTORY

Those inventories which do not fulfil the genuine needs of the production/operations process are classed under the general heading of corporate inventories. They are then accounted for separately and controlled against set targets. Typical examples of these categories include:

1. **Safety Supplies**. Inventory held as a safeguard against supply failure.
2. **Discount stock**. Inventory held above normal which has been acquired to gain the discounts involved.
3. **Slow moving**. Inventory which falls within that individual business's definition in this category.
4. **Marketing**. Inventory held as part of a marketing strategy (e.g., promotions).
5. **Sales**. Inventory held because actual sales were below forecasted sales, production having been made to budget.
6. **Policy**. Inventory held due to a corporate decision to make in advance of demand. This would be, for example, to supply spare parts, or perhaps in anticipation of material shortages due to likely external strikes.

PRODUCTION/OPERATIONS INVENTORY

Inventory is also held to fulfil a number of functions which are themselves necessary to achieve efficient manufacturing performance.:

1. **Pipeline inventory**. These exist because many businesses use external processes when producing the product or providing the service. The inventory necessary to transport products/services from one part of the system to the next is known as pipeline inventory. This is carried to cover the delay which occurs at each part of the system.

2. **Cycle inventory**. This is incurred as part of the rationale to produce in lot sizes. The trade-offs involved concern setting-up time gains and the order quantity to be made at each state in the process.

3. **Buffer inventory**. This is incurred to protect the business against unpredictable variations in demand or supply.

4. **Capacity-related inventory**. This is a way of transferring current work which is to be sold at some future period. Typical examples are finished goods made to meet a known seasonal pattern of sales.

5. **Decoupling inventory**. This provides the function of breaking the dependency of one part of a process with subsequent operations. This allows parts of the process to work at efficient levels, both being supplied from (and also supplying to) work-in-progress inventory.

At any one time inventory may be performing some or all of these functions simultaneously. In using these breakdowns as part of the basis for control, it will thus be necessary to assess how much of the inventory in question is there to provide for each function. This will be an arbitrary decision; the aim is not to generate statements of exactness but statements of magnitude. For, if the inventory holding in any one function is large, then it will demand the **corresponding level of control**.

Detailed inventory control

CORPORATE INVENTORY

Once the corporate inventory holding has been analysed, each inventory category should be assessed in terms of **what is currently held**. A realistic standard/target should then be set, and the inventory measured against new levels in order systematically to reduce this investment. As with other forms of inventory and cost, however, it is important to apply the 80/20 rule to ensure that the **level of control effort matches the size of the investment**. The 80/20 rule reflects the fact that, typically, 20 per cent of the corporate inventory categories will account for 80 per cent of the total value of corporate inventory holding. The key to reducing total investment is to concentrate effort on this top 20 per cent of items – and, hence, on 80 per cent of the total investment.

PRODUCTION/OPERATIONS INVENTORY

In considering the appropriate controls for production inventory it is useful to use the **dependent/independent demand principle**. This draws attention to the important distinction between items whose usage is not directly related to the use of other items (these are said to have an **independent** pattern of demand), and those whose usage does directly relate to the use of other items (these are said to have a **dependent** pattern of demand).

Small businesses are likely to have a mixture of both items, and will need to employ both systems. Finished goods are examples of independent items; dependent items include those components and sub-assemblies which go into finished goods.

1. CONTROL OF INDEPENDENT ITEMS

The essential nature of independent item control is the 80/20 rule. The procedure involves calculating the annual requirement value (ARV) for each item by multiplying annual usage by the unit cost. The highest ARV-ranked item is placed first, the second next, and so on (as for example, in Table 7.2). The rankings can be shown by way of a Pareto curve,[1] as in Figure 7.1. This illustrates the fact that the basis for control is to separate the items into the three categories referred to as A, B and C items.

A items are those with the highest ARVs (i.e., the top 20 per cent or so), C items are those with the lowest ARVs (i.e., the bottom 5 per cent or so). B items are those with ARVs between these extremes. The purpose behind this categorisation is to help distinguish between the type of control to be exercised. To explain how the control approach differs, Figure 7.2 summarises the key features involved in each of the three items.

The principle behind the control of A items is to calculate the reorder level involved (i.e., usage in the lead time,[2] plus as low a

---

[1] A Pareto analysis is a method of data selection which ranks the items involved in order of magnitude and separates the 'vital few' (classed as A items) from the 'trivial many' (classed as C items). The Pareto curve is an expression of this in graph form.

[2] If the weekly usage of a product is 60, and the time it takes to fill an order is two weeks then when the level of inventory held falls to 120 items, an order will be triggered off in the system. This quantity is known as the **reorder level**.

Table 7.2 A representative sample of 25 inventory items listed in order of decreasing annual requirement value (ARV)

Part no.	Unit value £	Annual usage (units)	ARV £ Actual	ARV £ Cumulative
C 120	16.90	1,500	25,350	25,350
A 190	61.50	315	19,373	44,723
E 060	5.25	3,440	18,060	62,783
A 207	12.15	860	10,449	73,232
D 180	11.50	750	8,625	81,857
C 293	13.95	430	5,998	87,855
B 140	9.00	450	4,050	91,905
F 095	6.80	450	3,060	94,965
C 290	8.50	315	2,678	97,643
B 110	10.16	250	2,540	100,183
D 217	8.90	280	2,492	102,675
A 097	7.65	315	2,410	105,085
A 521	3.80	400	1,520	106,605
A 584	4.25	290	1,233	107,838
F 110	1.10	750	825	108,663
C 256	0.75	500	375	109,038
B 296	1.10	250	275	109,313
E 115	0.85	315	268	109,581
E 163	0.25	630	158	109,739
D 301	0.63	200	126	109,865
F 180	5.10	20	102	109,967
A 050	3.60	25	90	110,057
B 320	0.30	300	90	110,147
B 340	1.50	50	75	110,222
D 060	0.40	150	60	110,282

level of buffer inventory as can reasonably be accommodated. Items are reordered on a frequent basis with great care being exercised to check stock levels frequently. Orders are placed when required and monitored frequently to ensure that no stockouts will occur, but to keep stockholding to a minimum. The associated clerical and contral costs will be more than met by the **gains on the inventory levels achieved and maintained**.

For C items the control principles are at the opposite end of the spectrum. Large buffer stocks are maintained and stock is replenished in large quantities and well before the stock held is likely to be used. The aim here is to maintain large stocks and to reorder well in advance. Minimal clerical support is required; this keeps clerical and control costs low when the ARV involved is relatively very small. By concentrating the business effort on the top 80 per cent of ARV, the **largest portion of inventory is thus given the maximum level of attention**.

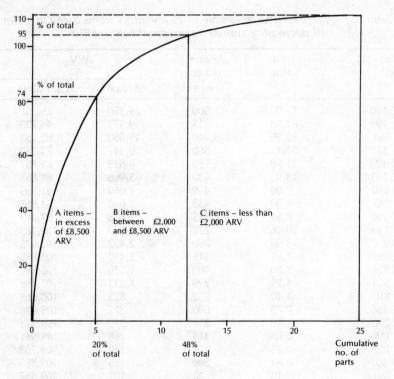

Figure 7.1   Pareto curve illustrating the 80/20 rule and typical A, B and C item categories

ASPECT	A	B	C
			ITEMS
Degree of control	High	Moderate	Low
Basis of control	Calculated		
		Past records	When needed
Records kept	Exact	Global	None
Level of buffer inventory	Low	Medium	Very high

Figure 7.2   General approach to be used for A, B and C item control

2. INVENTORY CONTROL OF DEPENDENT ITEMS

A dependent item is one that **goes into the manufacture of another item**. For such items only one forecast is necessary. It must be made at the highest level (i.e., where the items have an independent demand pattern) from which all other demands can be calculated.

The principle on which this information is based is called material requirement planning (MRP). The demand for independent items is derived from forecasts, known orders and inventory holdings. The calculated requirement is then exploded into the sub-assemblies and components which go into making a product. The quantities needed are then derived, net of inventories.[1]

For businesses without an MRP system, both the component and finished goods inventory levels should be controlled using the ABC principle.[2] Work-in-progress, however, needs a different approach. The first step involves analysing the inventory held throughout the process in relation to its position (i.e, where it is), the function it is providing (i.e, pipeline, cycle, buffer, capacity-related, or decoupling if it is production inventory, or the appropriate category if it is corporate inventory), and its value. This information will enable a business to establish where the high areas of work-in-progress inventory (£) are held, to assess the function provided and to set realistic levels for reduction. Again the 80/20 rule must be exercised to ensure that the high-value areas of work-in-progress are the ones which are monitored in order to make the biggest impact on the total inventory being held.

Once the high-value work-in-progress items are known, it is also possible to ensure that minimum lead times through the process are allocated to these items. What will happen is that these high-value items will be allowed into the system **with as little excess time as possible**. To ensure that they meet the schedule, however, they must be given priority throughout, thus reducing their time in the process (and, in turn, total work-in-progress holding). Low-value work-in-progress items, on the other hand, are treated in the opposite way. They are scheduled into the system **with an excess time allocation** and often with cycle inventory gains uppermost in mind. In this way, the work-in-progress inventory in question is allowed to travel through the process in a controlled way picking up functional advantages (e.g, cycle and decoupling) whilst attracting relatively low inventory investment.[3]

Just-in-time (JIT) production

The Just-in-time (JIT) production concept is an essential part of the management of some Japanese manufacturing companies. It is based

---

[1] MRP is a detailed control system. For those wishing to know more, refer to Orlicky, 1975 and Hill (1983, pp. 186–9).

[2] See p. 65.

[3] Elements of buffer inventory are also common in these two inventory categories. Its function is to provide a cushion against uncertainty of supply (components/raw materials) or demand (finished goods).

on a simple principle. The aim is to have all materials active in the process at all times thereby avoiding costs without benefits. The idea is to make finished products just-in-time to be sold, sub-assemblies just-in-time to be made into finished goods, components just-in-time to be made into sub-assemblies and raw materials to be delivered just-in-time to make components. The concept is very appealing. However, there are several prerequisites if it is to be achieved.

- It is most suited to high-volume manufacturing situations.
- It must be end-user driven. The business making the final products must take responsibility for instigating this development and liaise with its suppliers accordingly.
- Production schedules must be firm. If the material is not available in the system then production schedules cannot be increased.
- Suppliers must be geographically close to the customers thereby enabling regular deliveries to be made.

As a supplier you may be drawn into JIT situations with your customers. If, however, the above conditions are not met then inventory will have to be held (often by the supplier) in finished form in order to meet the JIT requirements. Of course, this defeats the inventory reduction aims which are an important feature of this system. The customer may reduce its own inventory levels but total inventory will not necessarily fall. It is important, therefore, to ensure that you understand the rules of your own application and the likely consequences for you if JIT is imposed by your customers. It is worthwhile to find out more about JIT at an early stage if developments appear to be moving that way.[1]

Conclusion

The control of inventory involves a complex set of decisions. These are made more difficult by the dynamic nature of the inventory movements, the multitude of parts involved, and its deceptive nature due to its omnipresence within a business. However, the stakes are high. Holding excess inventory (or allowing it to rise out of proportion with the business activity) can bring severe cash flow problems. The 1980s have brought a new awareness of the need to keep inventory under control and reduce it at every opportunity. A review of the seven companies looked at in Table 7.1 shows that some sound work in reducing inventory in the early 1980s had been achieved.

---

[1] For further details see Hill (1985), Schonberger (1982) and Vollman *et al*. (1984).

Table 7.3 Sales to inventory comparisons 1980–2 for the seven
companies in Table 7.1

Company	Aspect	1980		81		82	
		£000	Index	£000	Index	£000	Index
Tufnol	Sales	6,768	100	6,058	90	6,180	91
	Inventory	1,333	100	880	66	969	73
Bar Productions	Sales	4,423	100	3,916	89	3,623	82
	Inventory	810	100	531	66	515	64
Sandalin	Sales	1,333	100	1,103	83	1,758	132
International	Inventory	207	100	126	61	168	81
Copeland and	Sales	2,577	100	1,850	72	2,220	86
Jenkins	Inventory	272	100	218	80	184	68
Hayes, Ford	Sales	1,646	100	1,403	85	1,398	85
and Elliot	Inventory	320	100	290	91	236	74
Birmingham	Sales	965	100	621	64	702	73
Plastics	Inventory	128	100	118	93	139	109
Engineering and	Sales	810	100	884	109	809	100
Glassfibre	Inventory	129	100	119	92	89	69
Developments							

Source: Financial accounts of the companies listed

In six instances, the companies had improved the relationship
between sales and inventory during the period. However, in 1981
three companies had an adverse sales/inventory performance compared to 1980, which two then corrected by the following year.
Birmingham Plastics' sales/inventory ratio, on the other hand, deteriorated further in 1982 with inventory eventually up 9 points whilst
sales were down by 27 points compared to 1980. This overall check,
usually expressed as the inventory turnover ratio,[1] is a simple way of
calculating improvements on the use of inventory whilst providing a
monitor on overall investment.

Small businesses need to undergo some radical rethinking regarding the inventory levels held to support its sales. The pressure on
cash in the late 1970s – early 1980s has brought, in turn, a squeeze on
inventory. Businesses, such as the six improvers in Table 7.3 are
learning to work with reduced inventory holdings. It is important,
therefore, that when sales start to grow inventory is kept severely in
check. This will provide cash for essential investments in those other
areas, which are so important for overall business success.

---

[1] Inventory turnover $= \dfrac{\text{Cost of goods sold}}{\text{Average inventory}}$.

CHAPTER 8

How to Study and Analyse Production/Operations Work

Introduction

As explained in Chapter I, the POM task is to convert inputs into the required outputs of products/services to be sold in the market place. The prosperity (and even the survival) of a small business is largely determined by how well this is accomplished. Two of the most important features of the task concern the effectiveness of this conversion process and the achievement of the quality specification of the product or service. A key measure of effectiveness is **productivity**, the ratio between outputs from and inputs into the process. The achievement and improvement of productivity and the control of quality are important POM tasks, critical to the viability of the business as a whole.

Productivity

The basic concept of productivity is simple: **how much can a business produce (outputs) from the resource (inputs) utilised?** Or, conversely, how much resource is needed to produce the required level of products or services? Productivity is, therefore, the relationship of output to input:

$$\text{Productivity} = \frac{\text{Output}}{\text{Input}}$$

An increase in productivity can be brought about by either an increase in output or a decrease in input, in relation to each other. In this way it represents the key to improving business performance by lowering relative costs and thereby paving the way for more rapid growth, increased investment, higher remuneration and a better working environment in the future.

Trends in productivity over time show how efficiently all factors of output (capital, materials and labour) are being used. They will reflect the better utilisation of all resources brought about by improvements in many aspects including production/operations processes, equipment, planning, work methods and training. In this way, a business can improve its competitive stance and hence secure its present position and its future growth.

The need to be conscious of productivity and appreciate its vital importance in achieving a good overall performance is particularly pertinent to small businesses. In most instances these organisations do not have the specialist support functions whose job it is to concern themselves solely with a part of the total business perspective. And, as managers usually respond best to those challenges they understand, it is important that the productivity quest forms a significant part of the POM role.

How to measure productivity

There is no single, best way to measure productivity. The possible ways from which to choose need to reflect your business, and be taken over time in order to show the trends involved (i e., indexed over time against set goals), or how well you are doing in general (i e., compared to your competitors, or within your industrial sector as a whole).

The measures which can be used are of two types: partial or overall. Partial measures are often easier to develop and focus on some **specific aspect of the operation**. Care must be taken, however, to set these in the context of other measures which will provide different perspectives on the operations performance. The three most widely used partial measures are **labour, materials and plant productivity**. Each of these relates output (£value) to the hours and/or costs required to produce that output. Note, however, that it is important to ensure that the measures and improvements are directed towards those areas of significant costs (and, as shown in Chapter 4 and again in Chapter 9, in many businesses the higher costs have moved away from labour towards materials).

Overall measures focus on the effect of productive inputs on the **performance of a business as a whole**. One useful overall measure of productivity is that of added value.[1] This represents the difference between sales revenue and all the material and outside services' costs incurred in making those sales. Added value measures the wealth produced by the business, and by using this as a ratio against total employment costs, it provides a useful measure known as the **added value index**:

$$\text{Added value index} = \frac{\text{Total employment costs}}{\text{Added value}}$$

This ratio (often expressed as a percentage) is a valuable measure of management's performance because – unlike profit – it is less affected by factors outside a manager's control (e.g, inflation) and because it focuses on the key management task of total employee productivity.

It is important to stress the need to keep the measures you choose simple and meaningful and ones **on which you can act**. It is essential, therefore, that you discriminate between the important and less important, thereby devoting your attention to a few key controls.

Ways to improve productivity

The opportunity to improve productivity is there for any small business. However, this potential has to be **achieved by conscious man-**

---

[1] BIM (1978) examines current schemes operating in 14 companies and summarises the benefit's and problems.

agement effort, and the way to do this is to base improvements on sound analysis. Action based upon an analysis of the facts is the way forward. Analysis will enable the manager to identify those areas where improvements will result in the most significant productivity gains and the actions taken then will be based on a systematic, comprehensive and co-ordinated approach to this key task. Analyses and improvements therefore go hand-in-hand.

Most small businesses will work at the operational level in terms of effecting productivity improvements[1]. This is aimed at developing procedures and methods to make the best of technical developments. Productivity improvements can come from different approaches to reviewing work. These include trial and error, intuition, or a systematic and analytical review of the tasks on hand. It is this latter approach which will be described here.

Work study

The term work study is defined in BS 3138[2] as 'the systematic examination of activities in order to improve the effective use of human and other material resources'. Work study is an analytical and systematic technique – analytical in that it seeks factual answers to questions, and systematic in that it follows step-by-step procedures during the factfinding investigations.

Work study comprises two main elements: method study and work measurement. The first concerns the study of the methods used to complete a task, whilst the latter concerns the different ways in which the work content of a task may be measured.

Method study

Method study is defined in BS 3138 as the systematic and critical examination of the ways of doing things in order to make improvements.

The key words in this definition are **systematic** and **critical examination**. As mentioned earlier, a feature of a sound approach to productivity improvement is sequential analysis of the present situation. The procedure when applying method study is to follow this sequence:

1. **Select**. It is necessary, in order to gain the most improvement from the application of these techniques, to ensure that the **area of**

---

[1] Productivity approaches can be at the scientific, technical or operational levels. These alternative approaches are described and illustrated in Hill (1983, pp. 215–16).
[2] *Glossary of Terms used in Work Study and Organisation and Methods*, 1979.

Symbol	*Activity*	*Used to represent*	
		Material/document	*Person doing the task*
○	**Operation**	Material, product, or document is modified or acted upon during the operation	Person completes an operation or task This may include preparation for the next activity
□	**Inspection**	Material, product or document is checked and quality, quantity or accuracy is verified	Person checks and verifies for quality, quantity or accuracy at this stage in the process or procedure
⇨	**Transport**	The material, product or document is moved to another location without being part of an operation or inspection	Person moves from one position to another as part of the process or procedure without being part of an operation or inspection
D	**Delay**	Temporary storage or filing of an item Not recorded as 'in store' or filed and not requiring authorisation for its withdrawal	Person unable to complete the next part of the task
▽	**Storage**	Controlled storage, governed by authorised receipt and issue; document filed and retained for future reference	Not used
◘	**Combined activities**	To show activities performed at the same time or a person completing two tasks at the same time The example here represents a combined operation and inspection.	

Figure 8.1 Summary of the symbols used to complete process charts, and their different meanings

investigation will lead to the most gains. Time spent on selecting the area of work to be studied is seldom wasted. Things to look for are areas of low performance, low throughput, high or excessive costs or low utilisation.

2. **Record**. It is essential to record **all the relevant facts** about the present work method, both as a basis for later comparison and to provide the essential facts about what currently takes place. To help in this, charts are often drawn using the international symbols described in Figure 8.1.

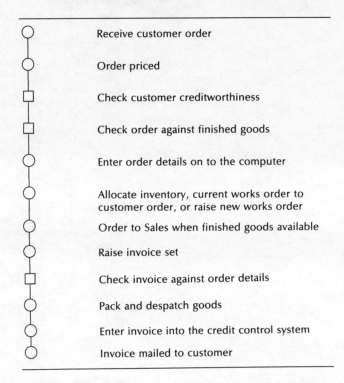

Receive customer order

Order priced

Check customer creditworthiness

Check order against finished goods

Enter order details on to the computer

Allocate inventory, current works order to customer order, or raise new works order

Order to Sales when finished goods available

Raise invoice set

Check invoice against order details

Pack and despatch goods

Enter invoice into the credit control system

Invoice mailed to customer

Figure 8.2   Outline process chart for a sales order procedure

These symbols are then used in the preparation of a number of charts which record the information in differing levels of detail. One analytical review is the **outline process chart** which is most useful for providing an overview of the procedures/operations involved in a business. This helps to clarify what is involved and also provides a priority list for future action. This chart records only the main operations and inspections involved in each procedure with a brief description, together with the time taken, if available. More detailed process charts can also be provided to show the movements of people, materials, documents or equipment using all the symbols given in Figure 8.1.[1] Figures 8.2 and 8.3 provide examples of an **outline process chart** and **multiple activity process chart** respectively.

In addition to process charts, another useful aid when reviewing a task is provided by the **multiple activity bar chart** which is used to detail the activities of two or more people/machines/pieces of equipment. Drawn against a timescale, the activities of those concerned are shown simultaneously to illustrate, amongst other things, the inter-relationship between them. Finally, a **flow diagram** may also be used

[1] See Hill (1983, pp. 222–5).

156

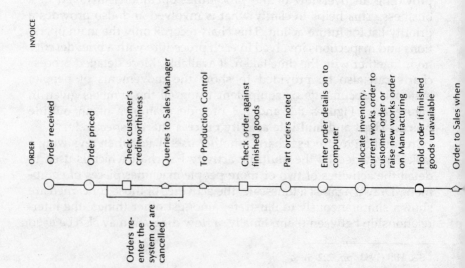

ORDER   INVOICE

Order received

Order priced

Check customer's creditworthiness

Orders re-enter the system or are cancelled

Queries to Sales Manager

To Production Control

Check order against finished goods

Part orders noted

Enter order details on to computer

Allocate inventory, current works order to customer order or raise new works order on Manufacturing

Hold order if finished goods unavailable

Order to Sales when

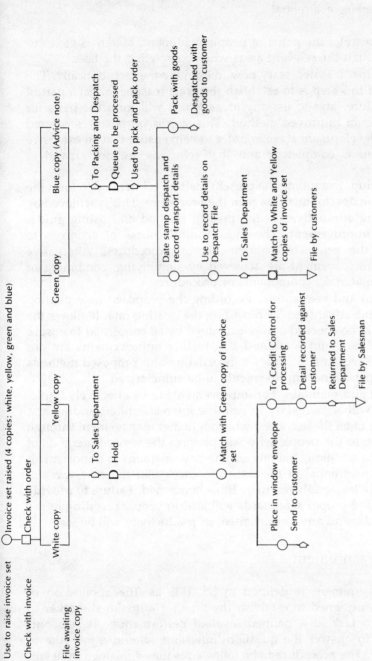

Figure 8.3 Multiple activity process chart relating to the outline process chart in Figure 8.2

to trace, to scale, the paths of people, equiment, materials or documents through the relevant areas when completing the task.[1]

3. **Examine**. It is necessary now to examine the facts critically. The purpose of this step is to **establish the exact reasons** for each part of the procedure, and to list any ideas which will form the basis for developing an **improved method**. This step is purposely separated from the development stage in order to help ensure that an extensive examination is completed, and that solutions are not arrived at prematurely.

4. **Develop**. Examining the present method is intended to form the basis for the development stage in the procedure. This is achieved by highlighting **alternatives** to the present method and listing **guidelines for improvement**. The most fruitful course of action is to eliminate the products, components or procedures. Alternative means of improvement are achieved by simplifying, combining or changing materials, components or procedures.

5. **Record and re-examine**. Recording the proposed new method has the same advantages as recording the existing one. It allows the proposals to be checked and re-examined by all concerned to ensure that the ideas could work and that further improvements are not available. Recording also allows the **existing and proposed methods to be compared and improvements to be summarised**.

6. **Instal and maintain**. For improvements to be effectively implemented it will be necessary to gain the interest, understanding and acceptance of all those concerned, from higher management through supervision to the people who will perform the revised methods of working. In addition, training on the new methods is important. It will also be essential in the future to check that the new ways of working are being adhered to by those concerned. **Failure to provide adequate and proper safeguards** will lead to people reverting to the old methods, and any improvement in productivity will be lost.

Work measurement

Work measurement is defined in BS 3138 as 'the application of techniques designed to establish the time for a qualified worker to carry out a task at a defined level of performance'. It sets out, therefore, to answer the question 'how long should a job take to complete?'. The procedure to be followed is now explained in detail.

1. **Select**. The first step is to select the task to be studied. The basis for selection depends on the ways in which the work measurement data will be used:

---

[1] See Hill (1983, pp. 224–7).

(a) Planning and scheduling work.
(b) Estimating and costing.
(c) Controlling labour and labour costs.
(d) Forming the basis of incentive schemes.
(e) Establishing delivery dates.
(f) Calculating future capacity requirements.

2. **Record**. All relevant details should be recorded about the study and filed when it is complete. Recorded at the top of the study sheet, they will include:

(a) Name and department of the person being studied.
(b) Description of the operation under review.
(c) A note of the working conditions at the time of the study.
(d) A study reference number which is the index for the filing system.
(e) Date.
(f) Start and finish time of the study.

3. **Analyse**. The purpose of the work measurement is to establish a time to complete a particular task. It is important, therefore, to ensure that the method being used by the person being studied is in line with the agreed way of working (if available), or is the same as the method which is being used on any earlier study. For it is on the basis of the method which is being used when the study work is completed that the **time allowed for the job** will be established. Any change in the method of doing the job should also require that the new method be remeasured and a separate time established.

4. **Measure**. Many small businesses will not have a special function with the necessary skills to provide the range of work study techniques. Whilst aspects of method study can be more easily self-taught, the selection and application of suitable work measurement techniques need to be handled with care.

However, having put you on your guard, let me now say that certain valid approaches to work measurement can be adopted and, with the principles governing sound measurement in mind, you will be more able to ascertain **what is appropriate and how it should be used**.

Techniques of measuring work

The key requirement in measuring work is to establish times to complete the tasks being reviewed which are **both fair and consistent**. To help meet this requirement it is necessary to recognise that the time taken to complete a task comprises three elements and all these elements must be taken into account when establishing the length of time it takes to complete the job:

- Work **directly** associated with the task on hand.
- Work **indirectly** associated with the task on hand (for example, collecting general materials from the stores or answering general telephone enquiries).
- A **rest allowance** to compensate for fatigue.

There are several different techniques that can be used to measure work and it is important to select the one which is most appropriate. In making this selection bear in mind that data on actual performance has to be collected in order to verify the time assigned to a task. Once verified, you are better assured that the times allocated are both **realistic and achievable** and, therefore, provide a sound basis for **costing, scheduling and planning purposes**.

LONG-DURATION, NON-REPETITIVE TASKS

If your business involves long-duration, non-repetitive tasks then the appropriate method to measure how long these take is one of the derivatives of estimating, explained below. Figure 8.4 shows the approach taken to determine the time for the same task using three methods:

1. **Estimating**. This technique involves establishing the time to do a job by assessing how long it would take based upon the **estimator's knowledge and experience of similar types of work**. It does not involve breaking down the job into elements, and so the estimate made is on the task as a whole.

2. **Analytical estimating**. This is a refined form of estimating in that a job is broken down into smaller elements of work and then the time required to complete each element is assessed, based upon the **estimator's knowledge and experience** (see Figure 8.4). In addition, the elements selected should, where possible, be chosen to form the basis for developing **synthetic times**. In this way, those elements of work involved in completing future jobs which are the same as the elements involved in previous jobs need not be estimated but can be allocated the time given to previous jobs (i.e., synthetically built up).

As in estimating, however, it is most important that the times actually taken when the job is completed are compared to the estimated times which have been previously issued. This is not only as a control but also to ensure that future estimates include these verified times as part of a formalised procedure and so help improve the accuracy of this form of work measurement.

3. **Comparative estimating**. This is also a refined form of estimating which requires that the work involved to complete a task be established by comparing the task in hand with a sample of tasks for which times have already been established. In comparative estimating, therefore, you need to determine a **number of job categories which reflect the work involved.**. These categories reflect bands of time (e.g., 1–2 hours) and **benchmark jobs** are agreed which fit into each of the relevant time bands (see Figure 8.4).[1] The other existing and all future work is then allocated to a timeband by comparing each task in turn with the benchmark jobs agreed. Each job would then be given the agreed time associated with the relevant timeband of the benchmark task to which it best compared.

In this way, jobs are measured by comparing like to like, which will include direct and indirect elements of work as well as variables such as skills requirements and unforeseen difficulties likely to be experienced when doing the job.

SHORT-DURATION, REPETITIVE TASKS

The most relevant way of measuring the work involved in short-duration, repetitive tasks within a small business is the use of **time study**. However, at the bottom end of the small business range it is most unlikely that a company would have (or could warrant employing) a work study or industrial engineer. It is more likely that specialists able to undertake this type of work would be employed in the larger small business.

To establish the time taken for a job will, therefore, require a different approach depending on the size of the small business. The following section shows these differences by describing the way a trained person would complete the task and then suggests some practical differences for the non-specialist to follow in a typical 'bottom end of the spectrum' small business.

As short-duration, repetitive work will usually be of a high-volume nature, it is important that the times established be as accurate as possible. This is because with high volumes relatively small discrepancies will lead to relatively large percentage differences and have a

---

[1] The recommended procedure for benchmark jobs is to establish or check the work content by a primary method of work measurement (e.g., time study) in order to ensure that the time band chosen is appropriate (see Hill, 1983, p. 246). For a very small business this may not be viable. In these circumstances, therefore, adequate checks need to be made although of a less formal nature.

TASK	ESTIMATING	ANALYTICAL ESTIMATING
Office cleaning	**An estimate of the time it would take** to empty all the ashtrays and waste bins, hoover and dust the office under review would be made. This would be based on the estimator's own past experience of similar work.	The tasks involved in cleaning the office under review would be broken down into smaller parts, for example: • Emptying 10 ashtrays • Emptying 10 waste bins • Dusting 10 desks • Dusting 10 chairs • Dusting 20 filing cabinets • Dusting 50 metres of skirting board • Dusting 10 window ledges • Dusting 5 doors • Hoovering 150 square metres of carpet with a high level of furniture congestion The next step is to complete an estimate for each of these parts. The individual estimates would be added to give an **overall time to complete the cleaning of this office**. Again, the times should be based on the estimator's own past experience of similar mark.

Figure 8.4   Types of estimating which may be used to determine the time to be allocated for completing the same task

profound effect on costings, price quotations, capacity calculations and manning levels. For this reason, therefore, a time for this type of work is developed by:

1. Breaking the job into **small elements**.
2. Measuring each element and rating the **effectiveness** of the work taking place (this includes speed and effectiveness, and is known as rating).
3. Adjusting the time taken to complete the parts of the job by

---

COMPARATIVE ESTIMATING

From past experience of cleaning offices, a number of job categories would be compiled by the estimator. These would be chosen to reflect the **different timebands of the work undertaken** (see below), and one or more **benchmark jobs** would be selected as being representative of each band. When selected, each benchmark job would then be analysed in greater depth, and a detailed study would be completed to check that the timeband to which each job had been allocated was **appropriate**. A full description of the individual tasks involved for each job would also be recorded, and filed for later use:

Timeband (hr)	Benchmark job(s)
0–½	Partner's office, 8 Southall Gardens
½–1	Purchasing Department, AB Imports, Floor 4, Bradley House
1–1½	Drawing office, Markham, Roberts & Co.
1½–2	General office, Housing Department, Bursley DC
2–3	Main open plan office, British Energy, West Midlands

And so on.

All future jobs would then be compared to each benchmark job and, usually, the midpoint of the timeband for the job to which it was most similar would be allocated and used in all the appropriate calculations.

Fig. 8.4   cont.

'normalising' the time recorded by the rating assessment which forms what is known as the **basic time**.[1]

4. Increasing this normalised or basic time by a percentage to cover other work observed which is of an **occasional or contingent nature**.
5. Increasing the time in step 4 by a percentage to allow for rest. This now constitutes the **standard time**[2] for doing the job.

---

[1] There are three rating scales in use in the UK. By far the most common, and the one suggested for use, is the BSI 0–100 scale. Step 3 involved adjusting the time to determine what it would have been if the person had been working at 100 or 'standard' rating.

[2] A standard time (see Figure 8.5) is the time which an average operator trained to do the job should take, working at 100 performance on the BSI 0–100 scale with due allowance made for the occasional and contingency work and an adequate allowance made to compensate for fatigue.

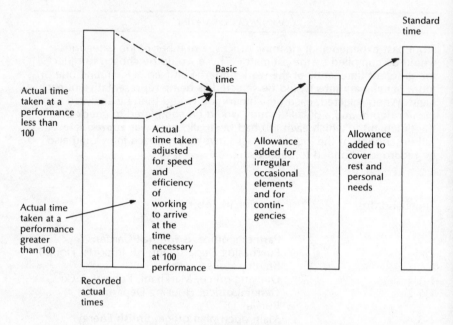

Source : Hill (1983, p. 250)

Figure 8.5   Main steps in the establishment of a standard time

Figure 8.5 summarises these steps as a way of explaining the procedure to be adopted. However, the detailed steps involved are far more complicated, as you would expect, than the outline procedure implies. For those businesses at the top end of the small business spectrum it is necessary for the production/operations manager to be fully acquainted with the established procedures to be followed. With businesses at the bottom end of the spectrum, the procedure to be used will differ in a number of ways.

PROCEDURE FOR THE LARGER SMALL BUSINESS

1. The first step is to gather **all the relevant data about the job** (including the method being used) and to record this on the relevant file and at the top of the time study sheet being used, similar to the example given in Figure 8.6.
2. Next, **break the job into elements.** As mentioned earlier it is important to select these with one eye on their use as a source of synthetic times which can be used in determining the time to complete other jobs which contain the same (or similar) elements of work. In order to facilitate the accurate timing of this type of

Department					Study No.				
Name					Date				
Payroll No.					Start time				
Study completed by					Finish time				
Operation					Elapsed time				
....					Ineffective time				
Working conditions					Net study time				

	(1)					(1)		
		(2)					(2)	
			(3)					(3)

Left-hand side of both sets of 3 columns: details of all repetitive, occasional
and contingency elements, together with any ineffective time observed
Column 1 : rating assessment for each element of work
Column 2 : actual or observed time for each element of work
Column 3 : adjusted time (known as the basic time) which shows the time it
would have taken if the person had been working at 100 performance on
the BSI 0–100 scale

*Figure 8.6   Typical sheet used to record background information on a
job being reviewed, and data recorded during a time study*

work, it is necessary to break the task into small elements, ideally
between 0.1 and 0.5 minutes each.

3.   Time each element of work **as performed by the person doing
this job**. Only trained people working in normal conditions
should be studied. It is at this stage where a study distinguishes
between **repetitive** elements (i.e., those parts of a job which
repeat regularly), **occasional** elements (i.e., those parts which do
not repeat regularly), and **contingency** elements. The latter are
tasks observed during the study which, though not an integral
part of the job being observed, do form part of the person's
overall job (e.g., talking to a supervisor about a general work
query).

   Details of the repetitive, occasional and contingency elements
of work observed during the study are recorded on a study sheet

similar to that shown in Figure 8.6. In addition, any **ineffective time** (i.e., time taken on activities which are neither part of the job being studied nor part of the person's overall work) is separated from the elements of work, detailed and the time taken is recorded in the appropriate column. These times are not rated, and therefore the actual or observed time is not adjusted at a later stage.

4. When timing each element, a rating is also recorded to reflect the **speed and effectiveness of the person doing the job**. The rating is recorded in column 1 of Figure 8.6, and the actual time taken, in column 2. Figure 8.7 shows some typical points on the BSI 0–100 rating scale.

5. Steps 3 and 4 should be **repeated over a number of working cycles** to complete the study.

6. The study has to be checked for accuracy and then the actual times need to be adjusted (or normalised) to the time it would have taken if the person observed **had been working at standard or 100 rating** on the BSI 0–100 scale. This is known as the **basic time**, or the time is said to be expressed in **basic minutes** and is recorded in column 3.

7. The study is then used as one of several to establish the **standard time** for the job in question. As a guide, each job should be studied at least three times and preferably by three different study experts on three different persons. When sufficient studies have been taken (note that if there are insufficient studies then a provisional time may be issued) then the basic times for each repetitive element (see Step 3 above) are averaged.

8. The next step is to calculate the percentage allowance to be given which reflects the amount of **occasional or contingency** work recorded (see Step 3 above). The way that this is done is to take out of each study those elements of work in these categories and to record them separately. The total of these is then expressed as a percentage of the total repetitive elements, with a small upward adjustment to allow for any unforeseen work of this type.

9. In a similar way, the amount of **rest allowance** to be provided for each part of the job is assessed using well established, rest allowance tables.[1]

10. The final step is to increase the basic minutes for each repetitive element, firstly by a percentage allowance for occasional and contingency elements and then by the percentage allowance for rest to give the **standard minutes for each element**. The individual standard times for each repetitive element are then cumulated

---

[1] Rest allowance tables have been established on the basis of scientific study – see, for example, ILO (1969, pp. 292–7).

RATING BSI 0–100 SCALE	DESCRIPTION	COMPARABLE WALKING SPEED (mph)
150	Exceptionally fast; usually maintained only over short periods of time	6
125	High degree of skill, co-ordination and speed; very fast	5
100	Average performance of a person paid on an incentive scheme; brisk performance of a well co-ordinated person sharing a sound level of skill Known as **standard performance**	4
75	Steady, deliberate performance reflecting the work rate of someone who is not paid on an incentive basis Hence, known as **day rate**	3
50	Very slow; distinct lack of speed; fumbling performance showing little interest for the task in hand	2
0	No activity	0

The rating awarded to each element of work will be in line with this scale, to reflect the speed and effectiveness of the work observed. Normally, people work in the range of 65–135 with most working in the range of 75–110. Usually, the ratings are taken at every five points on the scale

Figure 8.7 Some points on the BSI 0–100 rating scale, with descriptions

to give a **standard time for the whole job**. This – because it includes allowances for both rest and the non-repetitive work involved – represents the time you would expect a person working at standard performance to achieve throughout the whole of the working period. Note, however, that if the people working to these times are not paid on the basis of an incentive bonus then you should be looking for a 75 performance (i.e., day rate – see Figure 8.7). If they are working on an incentive scheme, then the aim would be for them to achieve a 100 performance rating over the working period. People who achieve more or less than 100 performance (i.e., standard performance – see Figure 8.5) will receive more or less bonus payments in line with an equal scale[1].

---

[1] A fuller explanation, including a worked example illustrated by the appropriate analysis sheets, is provided in Hill (1983, pp. 237–43 and pp. 250–53).

PROCEDURE FOR THE SMALLER SMALL BUSINESS.

At the bottom end of the spectrum of small businesses the procedure suggested is based on the assumption that businesses of this size will not have the inherent know how to apply time study, nor will it be worth their while developing a sufficient understanding of the procedure to be followed. A short-cut method is therefore suggested which uses parts of both estimating and time study. Its aim is to provide a systematic (although less accurate) method of developing the time to complete a short-cycle job. The steps involved are:

1. Establish the time to do the job using **one of the forms of estimating, or by timing using a wristwatch**.
2. When you are satisfied with the estimated or calculated time then **increase it by a factor to cover other work** (the equivalent of the occasional and contingency percentage), and for rest. As a general guide, use a 5 per cent increase for the occasionals/contingencies and a 12.5 per cent 'rest' allowance.
3. This will generate **a time for the job** which embraces the job itself, 'other work' and will compensate for fatigue. It will serve as a better estimate for costing, scheduling and capacity planning purposes.

Using standard times

Once standard times have been established, they can then be used to calculate capacity requirements, form the basis for labour estimates, be used in the calculation of individual, group or departmental performance and so on. An example of how this works in the calculation of an individual's performance is provided in Table 8.1.

The output produced by an individual within a given period (usually one week) is recorded on the shop-floor and the data are then used to determine that person's performance within the period under review. Equating each job by the standard minute content allows time to act as a common denominator. When compared with the hours worked, it provides a performance measure for those concerned.

In this period, the person completing these jobs recorded a performance of 95. This then gives a measure of efficiency and may also be used as the basis for an incentive scheme where an hourly incentive payment rate for different performance levels would first be agreed. The payment (in this instance at 95 performance) would then be made for each hour an individual worked at this level (41 hours in this example).

Table 8.1 Individual's performance: output within a given period

Products/services completed in Week 9		Standard minutes per unit	Total standard minutes produced
product reference	quantity		
110	10	16.0	160
125	4	25.0	100
016c	120	10.5	1260
142	2	60.0	120
206	1	45.0	45
115	10	30.0	300
170	20	17.5	350
		TOTAL	2335

$$\frac{2335 \text{ standard minutes}}{60} = 38.92 \text{ standard hours}$$

$$\frac{\text{Standard hours produced}}{\text{Clocked hours}} \times 100 = \frac{38.92}{41.00} \times 100 = 95$$

CALCULATING CAPACITY REQUIREMENTS IN INDIRECT AREAS

In office and other non-manufacturing situations, one important control is to monitor capacity requirements. As workloads may change it is necessary to monitor these in order to adjust the number of people allocated to the various functions. Methods which may be adopted include Variable Factor Programming (VFP) and Group Capacity Assessment (GCA). They are similar in approach and the differences between them slight.[1] In both cases, times are established by using predetermined (synthetic) sources, simple timing similar to that suggested in the last section, or estimating. When setting up this control, information on the number of tasks completed in a previous period is collected. When times for all jobs are determined (with a due allowance for rest included) a simple calculation (i.e., number of different tasks completed in a given time period multiplied by the time established for those tasks) will show the **number of people required to handle the work completed in the given period**. Weekly charts similar to Figure 8.8 are then drawn up, which measure the trends in work flow and show the number of people required to handle the throughputs involved.

---

[1] Hill (1983, pp. 248–9, 254–5) gives more detail on VFP and GCA.

Goods receiving stores

Day
Date

Tasks	Allowed time		Total	
	Minutes	Per	Items	Time spent
Deliveries received		delivery		
Requisitions processed		requisition		
Stock record entry (in)		delivery		
Stock record entry (out)		requisition		
Stocktaking		tray of record cards		
Rest and relaxation allowance		person		
Other (please specify)		actual		

Total earned minutes

Clocked time for the day   (hours)

Efficiency % $\dfrac{\text{Total earned minutes}}{\text{Clocked time} \quad \times 60} \times 100 = \dfrac{}{\times 60} \times 100 = \quad \%$

The allowed times (minutes) would also be preprinted on this type of form

Source : Hill (1983, p. 255)

Figure 8.8   Typical daily control sheet for an indirect function using data derived from VFP or GCA methods of work measurement

PRODUCTION STUDIES

One important way to verify that the job times are based on sound calculations is to carry out a production study. This involves monitoring the amount of work completed over a period of time (at least half a shift/day). This provides a way of checking that the **people working to the times can achieve a reasonable performance**.

Quality control

The quality of the products/services provided by a business is of paramount concern both to its customers and to itself. For small businesses, in particular, providing the required level of quality is an essential prerequisite for success. The rest of this chapter outlines some of the important aspects involved in quality control systems and procedures, and does so with one warning: the best systems and procedures in the world will not do any good unless everyone (and not just the quality control personnel) is convinced that **providing the products/services to the required level of quality is of prime importance to the success of the business**.

Responsibility for quality

The concept of 'quality' concerns the question of how well (and for how long) a product or service meets a customer's requirements. BS 4778[1] defines quality as 'the totality of features and characteristics of a product or service that bear on its ability to satisfy a given need'. Quality is achieved by two separate activities: product/service design and the production/operations function whose task it is to make or provide it to the design specifications.

The approach that will provide the necessary **control of product/ service quality** should be based upon a clear distinction between quality assurance and quality control.

1. The function of **quality assurance** is primarily to determine the designspecifications and establish the 'management' of quality and the appropriate procedures and activities to be used in its control.
2. The function of **quality control** is principally to carry out the procedures, checks and activities which have been determined as being appropriate for the achievement of the quality desired.

Introducing a clear distinction betwen these two separate activities provides the basis for determining the appropriate **responsibility and reporting relationships**. Quality assurance, therefore, should report outside the production/operations function (for example within the design, R&D, or engineering function). In this way those responsible for setting the specification and control procedures to be followed are still the custodians of quality assurance. However, the responsibility for meeting these quality requirements should properly be placed with those who are responsible for doing the work. Although developments over the last 30 years have tended to separate work and responsibility for quality, it is important to ensure that these are reintegrated, wherever possible, within a business. Table 8.2 provides a general overview, related to the type of process, of the typical responsibilities for quality control as they exist in many businesses today.

---

[1] BS 4778, *Quality Assurance (including reliability and unavailability terms)*, 1979.

Table 8.2   Responsibility for quality control and process type

Type of process	The task	Responsibility for quality
Project and jobbing	The task and quality are normally integrated in the skills of the person	Usually vested largely in the performance of the task or provision of the service Primarily the person responsible for this part of the process plus supervisory support
Batch and line	Work has been deskilled to reduce, amongst other things, labour costs inspection and later quality control introduced	Theoretically the responsibility is still vested in the person providing the task with supervisory, quality control and inspection support In reality, quality control and inspection are seen as being responsible for quality

Source: Hill (1983, p. 267).

Whereas the project and jobbing process both lend themselves to this task/quality integration, in batch and line the tendency has been to separate these two essential features of work. It is important, however, to redress this by ensuring that the **responsibility for both task and quality are vested in the person doing the job.** In this way, the attainment and control of quality – so critical to the success of the business – will be at the most appropriate point in the operations function.

Quality of design

An essential task in a business is to provide products/services to **meet a market need**. The procedure to be followed to achieve this is fourfold:

1. Establish the **exact customer requirements** in make-to-order sales or the **customer's perception of quality** in standard product/ service markets.
2. Embody these in the **product/service design**.
3. Detail the **product/service design specification**.
4. Prove this specification through testing the design itself and the capability of the operations process to **provide the desired level of quality**.

Quality of conformance

The second aspect of quality is the control of quality in the operations process itself, known as the quality of conformance. This aspect can be broken down into the stages to be undergone at each major point in the operations process. These points now form the sub-headings under which suitable procedures and controls are discussed.

PROCUREMENT

The checks on quality at this stage comprise two important aspects. The first is to establish authorised suppliers and the second is the detail (including drawings, specifications, material or process certifications, and source inspections) which needs to accompany the purchase order. It is also necessary to ensure that drawing or specification changes after the order is placed are fully documented. Other details are included in Chapter 9, on Purchasing.

RECEIVING

All parts, materials or services need to be recorded and then inspected in line with the procedures laid down by quality assurance. Where the parts or service are of a critical nature, then an organisation should insist on monitoring both the supplier's processes and their quality control procedures.[1] However, most businesses limit themselves to checking items or services once they have been purchased. In some instances this may involve only a quantity count. However, there will often also be a need to check the characteristics of a product to ensure that the delivery meets the specification. In these instances, it would be too expensive to check all items delivered and so **acceptance sampling plans** would be used.[2]

IN-PROCESS QUALITY CONTROL

The way a process or individual performs will vary. The key to in-process quality control is to know what the process is likely to do,

---

[1] A good example of this is the Ministry of Defence (MOD) which requires prime contractors to meet these type of procedures as laid down and administered by the Ministry. In the case of sub-contractors (often the more likely position for small businesses) the MOD have recognised a new scheme of assessment operated by the British Standards Institution (BSI) and based on BS 5750. (*Specification for Design, Manufacture and Installation*). Reading this will offer both marketing and quality contol insights for businesses in these types of manufacturing markets.

[2] See Hill (1983, pp. 280–3) for some typical sampling plans, and also Chapter 9 'Purchasing', p. 190.

or what it is doing. Furthermore, processes produce similar but not identical products; the variations which exist are, in fact, part of the process and are termed **assignable changes**. In addition, however, deviations from quality can be caused by **random changes** in a process. The key to quality control is to introduce a procedure which, based upon what is happening in the process, distinguishes between assignable and random changes, determines the source of the random change, and rectifies it.

The most appropriate point to control in-process quality is at the time the work is being carried out. In this way the nature of the quality is one of **measurement rather than control**, and allows for adjustments to be made before the process begins to produce rejects (or, at worst, soon afterwards).

Finally, it is important to ensure that quality control checks are made immediately before any stages in the process where high added value will occur. The reason is obvious. Compounding errors must be systematically avoided in order to keep reject costs to a minimum.

FINISHED ITEMS AND SERVICE/DELIVERY COMPLETION

The final step is the control of quality **at the end of the process**, including delivery and installation where appropriate. Depending upon the value and critical nature of the product/service then control based upon 100 per cent inspection or a sampling plan should be introduced.

Conclusion

The essential nature of the aspects of the POM task covered in this chapter cannot be overstressed. But the key management task is how to implement these ideas in order to achieve the productivity improvements and quality levels so essential to the success of a small business. Although the answer to this question has many facets, one of the most important prerequisites is **employee involvement**. Building on one of its inherent features, small businesses must capitalise on the opportunity to involve people – not just for itself but as the most effective and best value-for-money approach to improving the longterm success of the business. Unless a business taps the inherent ideas and resources which exist in the workplace, then not only does it fail to capture the use of this resource but (at best) will forgo the opportunity and (at worst) alienate and create resistance to change which will have serious repercussions on its rate of success. Treating people as responsible and resourceful contributors, essential to the viability and growth of a business, is rewarding for all concerned – the people, management and the business. Resistance to improvements often results not from the **nature of the proposal but from the style of its implementation**. Involvement is a key feature in the successful introduction of improvements and the assured quality of the products being made or services provided.[1]

---

[1] Lathan and Saari (1982) give details of the productivity improvements made (and maintained) by involving truck drivers and their unions in setting revised output goals.

Purchasing

Introduction

As mentioned in Chapter 4, the Census of Production reveals that for manufacturing companies of all sizes the cost of purchases in 1981 was 4.2 times greater than the wages paid to operatives, and 3.7 times greater than the wages and salaries paid to employees.

Not only is this a significant factor but a glance back at earlier years shows that the relative size of purchases is increasing (see Table 9.1).

To corroborate this, simply check your own expenditure breakdown which will, for the most part, show a similar pattern. The

Table 9.1 Ratio of purchases to costs of wages and salaries for
manufacturing industries, selected years

	SIZE OF PURCHASES RELATED TO	
Year	Operatives	All employees
1970	3.9	2.6
75	4.2	2.8
79	4.6	3.0
81	4.2	3.7

Source: *Business Monitor Report*, 1981.

conclusion to be drawn from this is fairly obvious – by getting the big items under control, the impact on your business will be the most noticeable. The aproach to achieving this is in three parts.

1. The cost reduction and cost avoidance techniques associated with **value analysis** and value engineering, which were dealt with in Chapter 4.
2. **Control on material usage** through better quality (see Chapter 8).
3. **Effective purchasing**, the subject of this chapter.

The right approach to purchasing

The biggest inhibiting factor which influences many small businesses in their approach to purchasing is that many people consider it to be an area of 'common knowledge'. This is derived from the fact that everyone regularly goes through their own personal purchasing routines. The danger arising from this is that the approach to purchasing within a business will suffer by being under-resourced, ill-defined and unprofessional. But given the size of the purchasing 'spend' and its impact on profit margins this cannot be allowed to happen. All too often it does; the opportunity offered for achieving the substantial economies associated with sound purchasing procedures is not fully or systematically exploited. Yet when (as is the usual case) purchases form a high percentage of total costs, a saving on bought-out items will result in an uplift in profits similar to that brought about by a considerable increase in sales.

In many small businesses, purchasing has the classic hallmarks of the 'cinderella function'. It is treated (and resourced) as little more than a routine clerical task, with many jobs being shared and with no overall policies being determined. The purpose of the rest of this chapter is to outline some of the most important procedures and controls involved in purchasing, and to stress the approach that should be followed.

Objectives of purchasing

The well-known definition of purchasing's objectives is 'to purchase the right quality, at the right time, in the right quantity, from the right source and at the right price'. However, this is a gross oversimplication. It involves in reality sets of trade-offs which need to be **resolved and agreed by the business as a whole**. A fuller set of statements (or objectives) therefore needs to be developed by each business in order to give more direction to the purchasing tasks. It will also be necessary for each business to decide on the degree of emphasis to be placed on each part. As a starting point, the following statements (or objectives) are offered for consideration.

1. To supply the business with a **flow of materials, components and services** in line with its requirements.
2. To provide **continuity of supply** by maintaining sound links with existing suppliers whilst seeking and developing other sources of supply, either as alternatives or to meet anticipated needs.
3. To obtain the best value for money taking into account aspects such as **delivery reliability and quality, as well as price**.
4. To ensure that information and advice is both provided to and received from other parts of the organisation to help the **effective operation of the business as a whole**.
5. To develop policies, procedures and controls **appropriate to the business** and in line with the foregoing objectives.

These statements are necessarily expressed in general terms – particular businesses must be more specific, and be prepared to quantify their purchasing objectives, whilst at the same time accepting the need for review against incremental changes in strategy at the product, market or manufacturing levels.

Purchasing procedures

All businesses need to purchase items as a necessary part of their activities. It is important, therefore, for a small business to set up appropriate procedures and paperwork systems to cope with this task. Before identifying the main clerical steps involved, it will, however, be useful to go through some of the more important overall procedures involved in this activity.

Buying agreements

The type of buying agreement used will depend not only on the items being purchased, but also the terms which can be agreed with the supplier. If your requirement is relatively small then the chances are that you will have to comply with the supplier's decisions.

SCHEDULED BUYING

The supplier is given an **estimate of the forecast requirement of an item**, and it is against the overall estimate of demand that a firm order is placed. Additional firm orders are made only as and when required. A supplier will often reflect the estimated total requirement discussed with the customer in the price and delivery commitments it makes. If actual orders fall well short of the forecasts then it is likely to sour future relations.

BLANKET OR BULK ORDER BUYING

A blanket or bulk order is placed to cover the **total demand requirements over a stated period**, to be called off against either an agreed schedule or on an 'as-required' basis. The supplier may manufacture the whole order at the same time (with the assurance that the buyer will accept the goods) or in line with the schedule. If the order is cancelled, the buyer must accept delivery of the completed items plus the work-in-progress at an agreed valuation. The nature of blanket orders qualifies them for high quantity discounts whilst the items are invoiced only against each individual order, with the risk limited to the size of each bulk order.

CONTRACT BUYING

Contract buying constitutes a **formal contract** drawn up between a supplier and buyer which specifies how and when deliveries should be made and paid for, the price, quality, cancellation agreements, the extent of the buyer's liability, and so on.

JOINT SUPPLIERS

Splitting orders between two or more suppliers may be justified through reducing the risk of supply interruptions and enhancing price competition. However, any **quantity discounts or reduced supplier commitment** to your business should be carefully weighed against these potential gains.

SMALL ORDERS

In order to reduce the time involved in purchasing and progressing small orders, one of several approaches may be used:

1. **Requisition/purchase order**. A combined requisition and purchase order is completed by the originator of the requirement. Copies go to the supplier, purchasing and goods inwards departments. This should be used only within clearly defined limits.
2. **Petty cash**. Small purchases are paid for in cash directly on receipt or collection of the items involved. Working within a procedure of receipts, this reduces the paperwork involved in these transactions.
3. **Telephone orders**. Small orders can often be effectively handled by telephone which, by using monthly statements, eliminates the need for orders and individual invoices.
4. **Cheque with order**. This method involves sending a blank cheque with an appropriate upper limit to cover small orders. The blank cheque would need to be suitably endorsed with a phrase such as 'not more than £x'. The supplier completes the cheque details and banks it as the goods are delivered.

Price agreements

Various types of price agreements can be made between a supplier and a customer:

1. **Fixed price contracts**. In a fixed price contract, the price agreed at the time of ordering will be the price charged.
2. **Fixed price, subject to adjustments**. This is a fixed price contract adjusted on an agreed basis to cover changes in labour, material and other specified costs. These are typically used where the contract is over a long time period or the material price fluctuates (e.g., materials, such as copper, bought on the London Metal Exchange).
3. **Cost-plus contracts**. In a cost-plus contract, the buyer undertakes

to pay the supplier's costs plus a percentage or fixed fee to cover profit margins. It is important to avoid the former of these (i.e., a percentage on top of the supplier's costs) wherever possible, because it gives the supplier a financial incentive to incur high costs.

4. **Renegotiable contracts**. A renegotiable contract is costed but includes a clause allowing the buyer to renegotiate the contracted price in the light of subsequent events.

Price analysis

Price analysis is the procedure involved in breaking down a quoted price in order to determine the reasonableness of the proposed charge. The procedure requires that the constituent elements of both cost and profit are analysed and a check on the level made, based upon:

1. **Previous prices** for the same or similar items.
2. **Estimates** prepared by the business's own internal section.
3. Cost information provided by the **supplier**.

The advantages which accrue from this analysis are not only of a comparative nature but also to provide the basis for negotiation, both now and in the future.

Obtaining quotations

Normally for all important items, quotations should be obtained before an initial order is placed. Repeat orders should be subjected to this procedure only annually unless there is a price, delivery or specification change by the supplier. A standard enquiry form similar to the one shown as Figure 9.1 should be used.

On receipt, the quotations need to be considered, and factors other than price taken into account, including:

- Quality specification.
- Guarantees offered.
- Supplier reliability (where known).
- Any suggested alterations to the requirement (for example, a trade-off between price and delivery volumes).

The information then needs to be summarised in order to facilitate an objective assessment of the quotations which have been received.

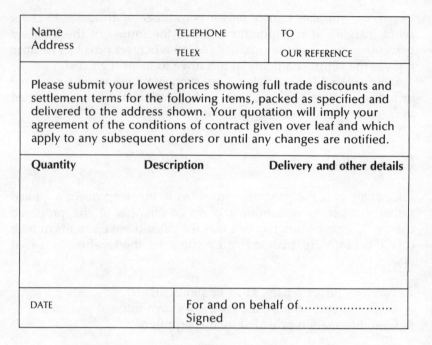

Name Address	TELEPHONE TELEX	TO OUR REFERENCE
Please submit your lowest prices showing full trade discounts and settlement terms for the following items, packed as specified and delivered to the address shown. Your quotation will imply your agreement of the conditions of contract given over leaf and which apply to any subsequent orders or until any changes are notified.		
Quantity **Description**		**Delivery and other details**
DATE	For and on behalf of .... Signed	

Figure 9.1   Sample enquiry form (not to scale)

Discounts

Price negotiations often include some element of discount agreed to cover one or a number of orders:

1. **Cash discounts**. Cash discounts are given against prompt payment of an account. Although this decision is one of financial rather than purchasing policy, liaison between the two parts of the business should lead to an agreed approach being taken.

2. **Quantity discounts**. In negotiations, the aspect of quantity discounts is an important feature in determining price. The discount may relate to single, scheduled or blanket order buying as explained in the section on buying agreements.

3. **Cumulative discounts**. Cumulative discounts are used to cover several situations:

  (a) Where the quantities required of an item over a given period **are not known**.
  (b) To gain the advantage accruing from the **cumulative spend** with a supplier.

(c) To gain the advantage accruing from **bringing together like items** and placing that business with the same supplier.

In each of these instances, varying discounts are agreed at different quantity or purchase value levels, with agreed settlement procedures. In addition, quantity discounts could also be agreed for item (c) where the cumulative demand over a number of items is assessed and a blanket order placed to cover a given period.

The purchasing cycle

This section outlines the procedures involved in the purchasing cycle from request to payment and will include samples of the paperwork involved. The cycle starts after the prepurchasing activities such as participation in design, and enquiry activities.

Phases in the cycle

We can isolate three significant stages here.

NOTIFICATION PHASE

The notification of the need to purchase will be in the form of either a requisition note (see Figure 9.2) or a bill of materials or a materials schedule, issued by the production control system.

ORDERING PHASE

On receipt of a notification to purchase, the buying function is responsible for checking its accuracy, its conformity to any standard specifications, previous purchasing decisions and how it relates to internal decisions, thus ensuring that tie-ups between departments have been made. If the item is standard, then a repeat order will be made, based upon previous decisions but bearing in mind the need to reconsider these periodically. If the item is not standard, then the enquiry/quotation loop will be triggered off before an order is placed.

The purchase order (see Figure 9.3) will go to the supplier with copies normally going to the goods inward and the requesting departments. File copies in purchase number order – known as the purchase order master file – and by supplier name in delivery date order will be

| PURCHASE REQUISITION | | | PR NO. |
| Please order the following | | | DATE |
Quantity/ weight	Stock/Ref number	Description	Price—unit weight

Deliver to		Date required
Order No.	Supplier	Signed
Date		Approved

Figure 9.2   Typical purchase requisition note (not to scale)

own business name

Form No.

B.T. HOUGHTON LTD
PURCHASE ORDER

Anchor House
Grace Road
Stoke-on Trent
ST1 4AW

Tel: 0782–56117/8
Telex: 472895
PO No. 80928
Date

Please supply the following to the above address

Quantity	Description	Price	VAT	Total
		£ p	£ p	£ p

Your quotation

Delivery requirement

Please mark relevant documents with PO No 80928 and acknowledge

For BT
Houghton Ltd

Buyer

Figure 9.3   Sample purchase order (not to scale)

kept in the purchasing function. The requisition will be cross-referenced to the purchase order and normally attached to one of the file copies.

POST-ORDERING PHASE

It may be necessary to progress an order to ensure that delivery dates are met. To facilitate this, the file copies of purchase orders, held by supplier's name and in delivery date order, are used.

Some suppliers send an advice note by separate post once the goods have been despatched. Where this happens, the relevant department and the goods inward function can be notified. On receipt of the goods, the quantity and quality will be checked. Where the check matches the delivery note accompanying the goods, you need to complete a goods received note (GRN) or just attach the delivery note to the GRN to save time and reduce transcription errors. If the delivery is not satisfactory, then the buying department can take up the complaint with the supplier.

The GRN is now sent to the purchasing department, who match it to the purchase order and, if complete, transfer the order from an 'outstanding file' to a 'completed awaiting invoice file'.

Later, an invoice for the goods will be received and purchasing's task is to verify the quantities and prices with the purchase order and GRN. Invoices are then passed through for payment, and the purchase order transferred to a completed order file.

Purchasing records

In addition to the documents and files described under buying procedures, there will also be a number of purchasing records which need to be maintained, of which the commodity and supplier cards are the most important.

COMMODITY CARD

The commodity card is a document which records details of suppliers, quotations, orders, receipts and other details for each commodity, together with references to the quotation's file.

SUPPLIER CARD

The supplier card records details of the orders placed for all items with a particular supplier together with receipts and references to the commodity card and quotation's file.

These two records, therefore, not only provide a cross-reference to the purchase order files but also allow an easy check on the state of an order whilst providing information which forms the basis for discount negotiations with suppliers.

Computers in purchasing

The procedures, documents and records described in the last few sections have been based on a manual system. During recent years, however, there have been developments in appropriate software to cover the basic procedures and records described here. The general advantages and points to watch for in using computers have already been covered earlier in the book (see Appendix, Chapter 6) and these relate equally to a purchasing application.

In addition, there are several specific advantages accruing from typical computer applications within purchasing which are over and above keeping records, handling transactions and providing up-to-date statements on outstanding orders or positional reports on each file. These advantages concern the provision of **additional information and consequent analysis** which is critical to the effective management of purchasing's strategic role in the business. The type of information/analysis which needs to be considered would include:

1. **Value of orders placed** in a period.
2. **Value of forward commitments**, by period.
3. **Current expenditure/commitment** against appropriate budgets.
4. **Value of business placed on any supplier** to date and to be used in the discount negotiations described earlier.
5. **List of suppliers, in order of total spend**.
6. **Outstanding orders** (by value and time) **on any supplier**.
7. **Updated expenditure** against capital projects.
8. **Overdue orders** from any supplier against agreed delivery dates.
9. **Delivery performance** of suppliers in past transactions.
10. Details of **outstanding orders**, by order number, part number, or project number.
11. **Items to be progressed**, by week number.
12. List of orders showing **late or ahead of time deliveries** against agreed schedules..
13. **Reject reports**.
14. List of **disputed deliveries**, by supplier.
15. List of orders for which an **acknowledgement has not been received.**
16. **Vendor rating reports** (see later in this chapter).

The different items in this list will have varying degrees of importance depending on the type of business. The analysis should, therefore, be the concern of the business manager/owner and be treated as an important factor in monitoring business performance at a strategic level.

What do you demand from a supplier?

The reasons for choosing a supplier will vary both by business and by product service. As a guide, however the elements which go into the choice can be classified into seven types, and the mix between the trade-offs involved has to be made in the light of each requirement. The seven elements for selecting suppliers are:

1. Available capability and capacity.
2. Price.
3. Delivery speed.
4. Delivery reliability.
5. Flexibility.
6. Quality.
7. Past performance.

Available capability and capacity

It goes without saying that available capability and capacity is a prerequisite for supply. **Finding new suppliers** is therefore an important purchasing task, and one measure of its activity. In a formal sense, it is necessary to cultivate market intelligence, consulting trade directories and manuals (e.g., *Procurement Weekly* or *Kompass*) which provide information on suppliers and also prices of commodities. Organisations such as the Institute of Purchasing and Supply, local engineering federations and chambers of commerce will provide relevant data. It can also prove useful to go to the suppliers of your own suppliers to seek advice on other sources and, when your quantities are large enough, to consider the possibility of direct supply.

The next question to resolve is the **trade-offs between single, dual or multiple sourcing** for reasons of price competition and security of supply. For many small businesses a better set of trade-offs will be gained from single sourcing. Normally, the order quantities involved are relatively small to the supplier, if not to you. Single sourcing, therefore, gives you some leverage which you would otherwise not have, as well as a way of demonstrating commitment to your suppliers. In addition, it enables you to forge longer-lasting relationships based on trust and cumulative goodwill, besides keeping tooling and/or clerical costs to a minimum.

Price

The issue of competing suppliers and its effect on price has already been raised under the last heading and was addressed (indirectly at least) under the section on discounts. The size of the purchasing spend is large (see Table 9.1) and a check on most small businesses will support these findings. However, low price is a trade-off with the other facets involved here. In addition to the points raised so far, there are two important additional contributions to price reductions:

1. All too often, purchasing functions are insufficiently active in seeking price reductions from existing suppliers, or finding alternative suppliers and hence **fresh opportunities to get prices down**.
2. **Prices are settled at the point of negotiation**, and this is at the centre of getting a good price. It is both an art form and based upon sound practice. Seldom do you lose out by saying 'no'. At worst, this will only result in you having to return to accept the original offer.[1] It is also most rewarding to go through an established negotiating procedure. In addition, it often pays dividends to invite suppliers to tender a second time once you have a 'feel' for the market or in line with your own price evaluation (see the earlier section on price analysis).

Delivery speed

There will be occasions when orders are placed with suppliers primarily because of the short time in which they can deliver. Although a business may decide to look to its suppliers to delivery quickly (to reduce stockholdings) or be forced into doing so (due to unexpected orders), by and large this should be avoided.

Delivery reliability

In order to avoid stockouts or the risk of being late oneself, a small business should rate the aspect of delivery reliability very highly.

---

[1] Lysons (1981, chapter 9) has an extensive review of negotiating procedure; see also Baily and Farmer (1983, chapter 12).

Some suppliers are inherently reliable and the purchasing function can contribute to punctuality by favouring these suppliers, by not ordering late, by not asking for the impossible and by progressing orders well ahead of time. Remember that **anticipating delays** allows for new plans to be considered. Last-minute scheduling or rescheduling is expensive, frustrating and potentially damaging to your own business.

Flexibility

Linked to the last two points on delivery is the question of flexibility. This refers to a supplier's ability to **react quickly to unscheduled demands**, usually brought about by unexpected sales or supply changes. If your business is based, in part, on its ability to cope with these changes then those suppliers who are flexible will be part of your essential purchasing know how. It will also pay dividends to explain this to your suppliers, in order to help them understand the importance of responding quickly.

Quality

The importance of quality is self-evident. Some of the approaches to help establish and maintain supply levels will be detailed later. Failure to meet the quality requirements will lead to a combination of delays and additional costs, besides the additional workload pressures which result. It is important, therefore, to work carefully through the process of translating judgements of requirement and quality into the more tangible form of a **specification**. A clearly defined specification is a prerequisite for establishing, controlling and maintaining the necessary quality levels of your purchases (see the later section on quality procedures and the specification).

Past performance

Checking the quality of incoming goods and services is not only a time-consuming task but also an expensive one. It is important, therefore, to recognise that all the items to be checked will not necessarily require the same level of scrutiny. The question is how to discriminate between different deliveries. Part of the answer is provided by **evaluating the past performance of suppliers** and adjusting the level of control activities accordingly (see the later section on vendor rating).

Knowledge of the **past performance of suppliers** (in terms of delivery as well as quality) should help in making the decision on where to place a future order. If other elements in the mix are similar, then a sound performance record in the past would usually sway the decision.

Quality procedures and the specification

When the product or service has been designed, the next step is to create a specification, defined by BS4778[1] as 'the document which prescribes in detail the requirements with which the product or service has to comply'.

What is covered will vary from product to product and service to service, but is of a technical rather than a commercial nature. It is important, therefore, that the purchasing function is involved in developing specifications in order to advise on supplier availability for alternative sources and the impact on price and availability of the proposals embodied in the specification itself.

The description provided by the specification can vary from a simple brand name for a product to a number of drawings and statements comprising exact detail and specified tolerances. Every purchase order must communicate to the supplier what is required, but the costs of preparing a detailed specification can be justified only when this requirement is critical, or the volume is great and the costs are high.

The quality of the goods and services you purchase depends on the processes used by your supplier. The ideal position would be to be able to review the processes being used, and so assess the capability of suppliers in terms of their ability to meet a stated need. However, many companies are reluctant to allow customers such access, especially in the case of small businesses which invariably do not have sufficient 'clout'. Most therefore limit themselves to checking items and services once they have been purchased, at the point of delivery. In many instances, this will be no more than a quantity count and a visual check for apparent damage. Even where a business does wish to check the characteristics of an item it will not normally check them all[2] – the costs are just too high. To overcome this, the principle of **acceptance sampling** should be used. Each acceptance sampling is designed to ensure that items do not pass into the process if an

---

[1] *Quality Assurance (including reliability and maintainability terms)*, 1979, Section 6.1.1. Note the twelve types of specification listed in Section 6.1 of the Standard.

[2] In general this is true, but in situations where, for instance, safety is of the utmost importance 100 per cent inspection will be necessary.

unacceptably high proportion of the order quantity falls outside the quality limits. Some of these plans call for single, double and multiple samples to be taken.

Sampling techniques are particularly appropriate when goods are delivered in large order quantities. To check every item would not only be expensive and time-consuming but the tedium would, in itself, lead to human error. This has resulted in the extensive use of sampling techniques based on the theory of probability. BS 6001 and 6002[1] provide a range of suitable sampling plans and details on how to use them.[2]

Vendor rating

'Vendor rating' is the term given to the evaluation of a supplier. It involves keeping records on the performance of suppliers both as an input into future purchases and as a way to establish the level of inspection appropriate to their past performances.

It is a simple but very effective piece of analysis, and one which small businesses could find very useful to employ. In essence, it allows you to review the **actual performance of your suppliers in a more objective way** by providing information collected over time and against agreed criteria. In this way, performance trends can be seen and, when they fall below the required standard, be taken up with the supplier concerned, or form the basis for deciding to seek an alternative source.

A supplier's **quality performance** is assessed by monitoring the number of reject batches over a period. BS6001[3] provides for:

1. Normal inspection.
2. Tightened inspection.
3. Reduced inspection.

Each supplier, for each item they supply, is placed into one of these categories. Typically, for one item a company may start on normal inspection. If (say) any three of seven successive batches are rejected, then future deliveries of the item from this supplier would go on to tightened inspection. When seven successive acceptable batches were received, the level of inspection would revert to normal. If after

---

[1] BS 6001 (*Sampling Procedures and Tables for Inspection by attributes*) (1972) and BS 6002 (*Specification for Sampling Procedures and Charts for Inspection by Variables for Per Cent Defective*) (1979) include single, double and multiple sampling plans.
[2] Further details are also given in Hill (1983, chapter 10).
[3] BS 6001 (1972) provides a range of suitable sampling plans and illustrates the use of vendor rating within this approach.

fourteen successive deliveries a supplier was still on the tightened inspection then the position would be investigated further.

Another system would be to plot the percentage of deliveries rejected against the sampling plan, and to monitor adverse trends. **Norms and warning levels** would need to be assessed and established here.

A supplier's **delivery performance** can be monitored by awarding appropriate gradings to suppliers in terms of the number of late deliveries, degree of lateness, and the amount of expediting required.

Similarly, a delivery performance chart can be maintained which shows the percentage of late deliveries and the cumulative days of lateness over a given period.

Service performance is a way of assessing the amount of technical help and support given by suppliers, their willingness to provide such help and the general attitude displayed by them when the need arises. This could be completed by awarding a range of points against relevant vendor characteristics such as:

1. Technical know how.
2. Availability and level of technical support.
3. Level of field service.
4. Degree of co-operation displayed.
5. R & D capability.
6. Level of new product development.
7. Readiness to accept responsibility.
8. Advice on potential problems.
9. Kind and form of warranty offered.
10. Speed with which replacement items delivered.

Overall performance, would help to provide a total assessment of suppliers. This would need to take into account the three factors already described as well as the price. Starting with a maximum rating of 100, weightings would be given appropriately to the four factors of quality, delivery, service and price and then the individual performance within each category calculated. The total points awarded would provide a guide to the relative overall performance of each supplier.

Purchasing controls

For monitoring the purchasing function's performance over time, some useful controls are available. These take several forms, and it is important to select those which are the most appropriate for your business:

1. **General reports**. There are several general reports which should regularly be provided by purchasing to show the performance of suppliers, either in terms of trends or against agreed norms. The content of these will reflect the function's **own internal monitoring systems**.

2. **Specific reports**. Periodically, reports should be presented to reflect specific activities. Typical of these would be cost-saving projects, ones showing the number of price increases or decreases for a period, and the **variances between actual and budgeted overall material prices** for the period and on a cumulative basis.

3. **New suppliers**. A useful measure of purchasing activity is a statement of the new suppliers **found and being used** over a period.

4. **General market intelligence**. Monitoring relevant information provided to functions inside the business is another way of assessing the level of purchasing activity.

5. **Ratios**. These show the relationship between two variables, and can be used to show trends, set standards and provide measures of efficiency. Useful ratios to measure and control purchasing performance include:

(a) $$\frac{\text{Operating costs of the purchasing department}}{\text{Total value of purchases}}$$

(b) $$\frac{\text{Operating costs of the purchasing department}}{\text{Number of orders placed in the period}}$$

(b) shows the average costs of placing an order and should be used in conjunction with (a).

(c) $$\frac{\text{Value (£) of purchase orders placed in the period}}{\text{No. of purchase orders placed in the period}}$$

(c) reveals the average value of the purchase orders placed in a period. Note, however, that this figure can be distorted by a change in order mix.

(d) $$\frac{\text{Value of purchase savings in the period}}{\text{Value of purchase orders placed in the period}}$$

(d) is a statement of the purchase savings reported, expressed as a percentage of the total purchases placed. For this to be a true measure of purchasing performance the savings must be **directly attributable to purchasing activities** – for example, lower prices negotiated by the buyer, changes in supplier which have led to a decrease in prices, and changes in ordering practice (e.g. combining orders) which have led to reduced prices.

Conclusion

On the face of it, many small businesses do not have a strong bargaining position when it comes to purchasing. However, it is important that a business attempts to get the best it can by maximising its purchasing effort and playing to its strengths. At the bottom end of the small business sector it will often be the owner of the business himself who does the purchasing. It is important, therefore, for him to exploit the advantages of his position by carefully evaluating the level of product commitment he can make, in terms of order size, continuity and payment. Similarly, local business contacts may provide the opportunity for a number of companies to combine together on the purchasing of common items in order to enhance the possibility of discounts and delivery reliability.

Most businesses, no matter how small, will have some strengths. These must be **first recognised and then exploited** wherever possible by tireless bargaining – the pickings can be large indeed!

CHAPTER 10

Payment Systems and Employee Policies

Introduction

This chapter deals with payment systems and employee policies for those people who are (or who traditionally have been) paid on an hourly basis; it concludes with a short section on management succession. It is opportune, therefore, to comment at the start upon the importance of pay to an hourly-paid person, in order to highlight the significance of this factor in terms of job interest and motivation. Although recently researched views have clearly indicated that pay levels are not a major factor in the motivation of people, it is important to place this in context. Much of the research work on which these findings were based involved salaried staff whose opportunity for job interest and advancement was very different from that afforded to hourly-paid persons. 'Transposing' these results should be done only with great care. For the hourly-paid person pay is important, and the wage system should not be lightly changed.

This chapter is designed to provide insights into alternative approaches in the areas of payment systems and employee policies, in order to provide the basis on which to make a more informed decision.

Wage payments

There are two aspects to wage payments. The first concerns the **actual value**, the second concerns the **relative value** of the wage rate. Actual values deal with the hourly rate of pay which goes with the job, and comprise both a finite (the actual amount) and a relative (compared to other businesses) element. The relative value also concerns comparing one job with another inside the business itself.

An overlap between these two dimensions is clearly present – for instance, the degree of pressure on relative values will be affected by the level of actual values at the time. Actual values are determined by each business on a regular basis. They take into account factors such as wage rates and the state of the business. Each small business will have (and should know) its own set. This section will not deal with the factors to be considered in establishing actual values, and will cover only the relative value components of wage payments and the relevant approaches to be used.

Informal systems

Many small businesses use one or a combination of informal systems, in order to assess the relative importance of one job as opposed to others. These informal systems will have developed over time and will be based (as often as not) on market conditions, local bargaining and perhaps the historical value of jobs both in the business itself and in the local community. These informal approaches lack any element of systematic review and often result in pay rates which do not match the relative value of the jobs concerned.

In order to minimise the emergence of pay anomalies between one job and another, it is important for a small business to adopt one of the formal systems which are available and for that system to be in line with the organisation's needs.

Formal systems

The formal systems available fall under the generic definition of 'job evaluation'. The aim of these methods is to **rank the jobs in order of importance**. When this task is completed, the next step is to award rates of pay appropriate to each job grade.

There are two types of job evaluation system: non-analytical and analytical. For many small businesses, especially those at the lower end of the spectrum, one of the non-analytical forms will be more appropriate. The reason for this is that the high maintenance costs associated with the analytical forms of job evaluation will outweigh the gains which will accrue.

NON-ANALYTICAL METHODS

Job ranking is the most straightforward method of job evaluation. This involves assessing the importance of each job both as a whole and in relation to all other jobs. Working on their knowledge of the jobs (and supported by a job description) the assessors compare one job with all others and decide if it is more, less or equally demanding. The jobs are then ranked in an agreed order.

In a small business at the lower end of the spectrum, one list could cover all jobs. At the top end, it would be better to prepare a list for each department and then assess these across functions to provide an overall list for business.

Paired comparisons is similar to job ranking. Jobs are awarded 2,1 or 0 points, depending upon whether they are more, equally or less demanding than each other job. The total scores then form the basis for the rank list.

Job grading requires that before any job evalution is carried out, the number of grading levels to be used is agreed. The criteria for determining the content and type of the work in each grade are then defined. For each level, one or two benchmark (that is typical) jobs are chosen. For them, job descriptions are prepared. The jobs under review are then compared to the benchmark jobs and slotted into the grading structure. It is worthwhile when employing this method to also use one of the two previous methods as a check on the results obtained.

ANALYTICAL METHODS

The two principal analytical methods are factor comparison and points rating. These methods are not considered to be appropriate for use in a small business due to the specialised knowledge required and the expense of their implementation and maintenance.[1]

Incentive payments

Job evaluation methods concern ranking the relative worth of jobs to provide the foundation on which to base appropriate wage rates.

---

[1] They are not discussed here; consult Hill (1983) and Palterson (1967;1972) for further details.

Many small businesses may also wish to consider methods of providing incentive schemes which will reward effort by financial payment. For those who so wish, there are two broad categories of schemes to consider: individual/group incentives and company-wide schemes.

Individual/group incentive schemes

Later in this section, the types of schemes which small businesses might find suitable are described. First, however, it will be useful to comment upon the advantages and disadvantages of individual and group schemes. Individual schemes are those in which each individual is rewarded directly for his or her level of effort. Group schemes are based upon the efforts of two or more people with the rewards reflecting the joint efforts involved and without differentiating between each person's contribution. Whilst both have their own relevant application, individual schemes may result in higher productivity by encouraging each individual to work his or her own optimum level. Group schemes may result in disagreement within the group – for example, about 'pulling one's weight' and the relative efforts of the individual concerned. However, the trend is towards group schemes and these have a particular relevance to small businesses, especially those at the lower end of the spectrum. The principal reason is that they can help to reinforce the business identity advantage inherent in small size and the congruent nature of their contribution to the goals of the business.

Research in Sweden during the period 1965–80, based on a sample of companies with 50 employees or more, revealed that the application of group incentives rose by a half (from less than 40 per cent to about 60 per cent) whilst in the same period the use of all types of incentives fell from around 70 per cent to just over 50 per cent.[1]

TYPES OF SCHEMES

The traditional form of payment for hourly-paid or equivalent employees were either piecework or fixed hourly rates. Strictly speaking, piecework is the expression used to cover any scheme in which those involved are paid **only for work completed**. No work completed means no pay. Typical examples are in the payment of homeworkers, where a money value is given for each item assembled, or for a page of typing completed.

---

[1] Flykt (1980, pp. 318–26).

In the case of a fixed hourly rate system, payment would be at an agreed rate per hour, irrespective of the amount of work completed. These are typical payment systems for indirect and clerical staff.

For small businesses which wish to reward effort in the form of measurable output, a typical incentive scheme would be a hybrid of the piecework and fixed hourly rate forms. These types of schemes are based upon measuring the performance of those involved by expressing **actual standard of hours of work** produced as a percentage of attendance or clocked time. We can consider two typical schemes in more detail.

1. **Straight, proportional schemes**. A straightline, proportional scheme is represented in Figure 10.1.

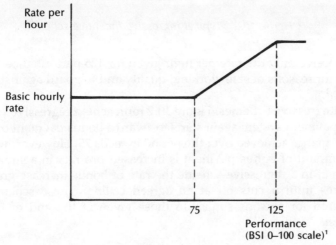

Figure 10.1   Typical straightline, proportional incentive scheme

In this type of scheme, a person who achieves a 75 performance or below will be paid at the basic hourly rate for the period concerned. However, those who achieve a 76 performance or higher are then paid at an enhanced rate per hour which comprises the basic rate plus an agreed bonus payment for performance achieved. The amount of bonus per point on the performance scale above 75 is agreed. It is represented in Figure 10.1 by the slope of the line between the 75 and 125 performance points. The difference in the amounts awarded (i.e, the slope of the bonus line) is known as **gearing**.

In this example, bonus payments have a ceiling, shown at the 125 performance point. This means that performances of 126 and above

---

[1] See Figure 8.7 on page 167 for details of the BSI 0–100 scale.

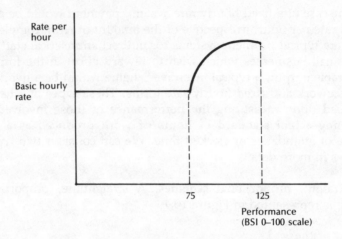

Figure 10.2   Typical regressive incentive scheme

will receive only the rate per hour given for 125 performance. This is done for reasons of safe working, quality and to guard against 'loose' times.[1]

2. **Regressive Schemes**. Figure 10.2 represents a regressive scheme. This payment system again starts to award a bonus payment once the performance achieved over the period exceeds 75. However, whereas the amount of bonus payment is increased pro rata in a straightline scheme, in a regressive scheme the rate of bonus increase gradually reduces until it cuts off at an agreed ceiling. These schemes are favoured for reasons similar to those given at the end of the last section.

FIXED HOURLY RATE V. INCENTIVE PAYMENTS

Many companies report that when they change the pay system from one incorporating an incentive element to a fixed rate scheme there is a fall off in productivity of some 10–15 per cent. Work done by Sven Flykt in Sweden and based on a study of a number of small industrial businesses with 50 or more employees support this. The results are given as Figures 10.3, 10.4 and 10.5.[1] It is important, therefore, to take these problems into account.

---

[1] 'Loose' is the description given to a time when it is higher than that necessary to complete the work involved. See also Chapter 8 for details on standard times and BSI 0–100 rating scale.

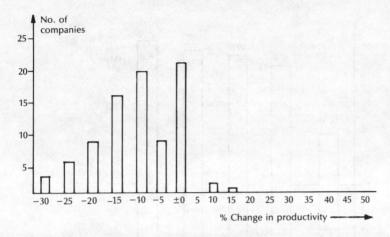

Source: Flykt, 1980
Figure 10.3   Number of companies reporting various levels of productivity change when going from an incentive to a fixed wage system (sample:82)
Note that the average value (−9.2) has been affected by a large group of companies who scored 0. Most of these have scored 0 because they now do not have any kind of follow-up of productivity changes, and in reality may belong to the 'don't know' group

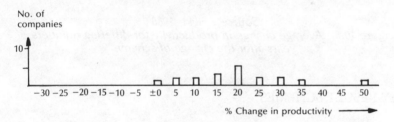

Source: Flykt, 1980
Figure 10.4   Number of companies reporting various percentage changes in productivity when going from a fixed wage to an incentive schemee (sample:19)

Company-wide schemes

Company-wide schemes for small businesses have the advantage of being able to highlight the **key result areas** of a business. They involve all the people employed and reflect the performance of the business as a whole.

---

[1] Flykt, 1980.

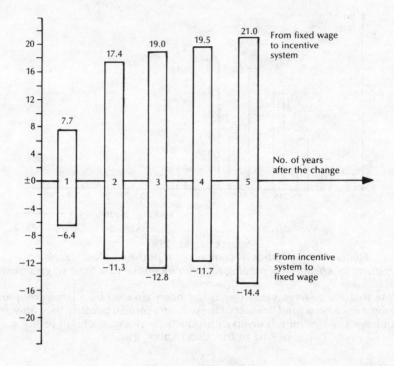

Source : Flykt, 1980
Figure 10.5   Average change in productivity for differing numbers of years after the change of scheme

KEY RESULT SCHEMES

The schemes described earlier under the headings of 'straightline proportional' and 'regressive', were based solely upon an assessment of the **actual level of output achieved compared to the standard level of the output target**. However, many small organisations will often wish to reflect other characteristics of performance which more closely fit the key result areas of their business. As with all payment schemes, it is essential to adapt them to your own company and to keep them simple. A distribution business, for example, may wish to include the following factors in an incentive scheme involving all employees:

- Output performance $= \dfrac{\text{Standard hours of all work completed}}{\text{Clocked time}} \times 100$

- On time despatches $= \dfrac{\text{Despatches on time}}{\text{Total despatches}} \times 100$

- Stock turnover $\quad = \dfrac{\text{Month's sales (£)}}{\text{Average monthly stock (£)}}$
- Correct despatches $\quad = \dfrac{\text{Despatches without errors}}{\text{Total despatches}} \times 100$

Goals for the selected performance factors are then set. Achievement of the goal gives a factor of 1. The percentage is then related to a scale, an example of which is shown in Table 10.1. It is important that the goals are realistic both in terms of **achievement** and **business needs**. As these are the factors weighting the final performance achievement, they need to be carefully considered. Being to 'loose' or too 'tight' will defeat the object of the scheme.

Table 10.1   Relating performance to a scale (extract)

	FACTOR WEIGHTING	% ON TIME DESPATCHES	STOCK TURNOVER	% CORRECT DESPATCHED
	0.80	82	5.6	91
	0.85	83	5.7	92
	0.90	84	5.8	93
	0.95	85	5.9	94
GOAL	1.00	86	6.0	95
	1.05	87	6.1	96
	1.10	88	6.2	97
	1.15	89	6.3	98
	1.20	90	6.4	99

If the output (number of deliveries received, despatches made, and so on) performance over the period was 90[1] and the other factors were 83, 5.9 and 96 respectively then the overall performance would be calculated by multiplying the 90 performance by 0.85, and 0.95 and 1.05 respectively. The adjusted figure would then be related to a bonus table and the rate of earnings read off and used as the basis for the incentive earnings calculation. It is important in constructing the bonus table that cut-off or regressive principles are considered, for the reasons given earlier.

COMPANY PERFORMANCE SCHEMES

Company performance schemes are not an integral part of payment schemes as such. They are more in the nature of a profit-sharing scheme, and so their effectiveness will, in part, depend upon the wage systems to which they have been added.

---

[1] See page 169 where the calculation of performance is explained.

1. **Priestman scheme**. In this scheme, a **total output figure for the business** is first agreed. If the output exceeds this, a bonus payment is made against an agreed scale. When this ratio exceeds a previosuly agreed norm, a bonus is paid to all employees against the set scale.

2. **Profit-sharing schemes**. In profit-sharing schemes, a bonus is paid based on the **profits made above a certain level**. A bonus payment in cash may be made, or (as often better reflects the cash needs of the small business) it can be converted into shares.[1]

3. **Added value schemes**. In added value schemes a payment is made based on the **overall performance of the business against an agreed ratio** which will involve added value as one factor. Added value (£s) is (sales–material and outside service costs), and is a measure of the wealth produced by a business. A typical ratio used in such a scheme is:

$$\frac{\text{Added value}}{\text{Wages and salaries}}$$

Employee policies

In this section, two important aspects concerning a small business will be discussed. The first concerns the ways of structuring work; the second looks at the issues and problems surrounding management succession, both in general and in relation to POM.

Structuring work

Paradoxically, one of the inherent strengths of a small business is its size. Small size affords an opportunity to provide work which is meaningful both in itself and in relation to the success and welfare of the business as a whole. Structuring the work will need careful thought to ensure that this opportunity is not missed, and that the link between the choice and the achievement of the business aims is not overlooked. Traditionally many businesses (especially as they grow) have sought to control their activities by such means as:

1. **Introducing specialists**, which has resulted in the activities of existing line functions being transferred to the control of (and management by) support functions. Several drawbacks to this

---

[1] See also Marsumoto (1983) for an interesting approach which also incorporated this idea.

approach and its consequences have been experienced. High amongst these are that certain tasks best executed in the line function are increasingly performed elsewhere. This means that the users of the systems or procedures are not the owners or developers of these activities. This is partly due to the manner in which the developments are introduced and partly because usually none of the specialists report directly to the user. Responsibility for the different aspects of the task is not adequately clarified, and this leads to later problems.

2. **Attempting to monitor activites in great detail** rather than providing those responsible for completing the task with the information necessary to make decisions about (for example) which jobs should be done first to satisfy the delivery requirements of the customers.

In addition, many businesses as they grow will move towards specialisation of labour. In this way the 'doing' task becomes separated from the 'planning' and 'evaluating' tasks. This has not only led to a situation where the person doing a job no longer considers that evaluation (e.g., responsibility for quality) is an integral part of the task; it has also meant that the job itself becomes less interesting.

In order to create a work situation which increases the contribution of the 'doers' and provides them with a meaningful set of tasks, it is helpful to consider:[1]

- Using small, **self-managed work groups**.
- Providing tasks which have sufficient job scope to be **interesting in themselves and identifiable with the business**.
- Allowing the group to **plan and evaluate their own work** on a day-to-day basis.
- **Integrating specialists back into the line functions**.

Management succession

PROBLEMS IN PRACTICE

The succession of key executives in a small business is critical. In 1971 a study[2] revealed that management succession in small firms almost equalled financial failure as the major cause of firms ceasing to exist as independent organisations. However, succession is not simple. It involves conflicting pressures and interests from those involved.

---

[1] See Schumacher's work structuring principles in his unpublished papers, 1979–81 and Hill (1983, pp. 315–27)
[2] Merrett – Cyntiax, 1971.

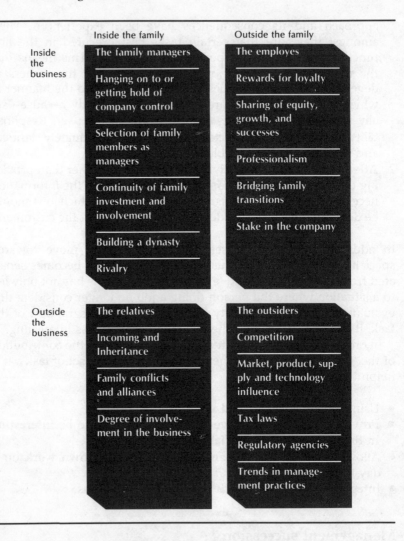

Source : Barnes and Hershon, 1976
Figure 10.6   Pressures and interests in a family business

Figure 10.6 outlines some of these conflicts and should help to sharpen awareness of the differences by providing four separate perspectives which may exist within a family business.

Figure 10.6 helps to indicate the diverse interests and preoccupations which exist in varying degrees, and the viewpoints held by different age groups. The segments show the different nature of the perspectives which may be held by family managers and employees, and the overriding difficulty for 'intruders' in bridging the 'family transitions'. It reveals the nature of the classic problems which often exist between the older and younger generations within the family managers' group, and the difficulties experienced at the operational level. These result from 'older-generation employees' in positions of authority (often the reward for loyalty, past performance and personal growth linked to the growth of the business) and 'younger-generation employees' pursuing values of professionalism and expertise, seeking opportunities for growth and 'reasons for staying' criteria.

PREPARING FOR CHANGE

Within the overall context of management succession, one of the most important transfers of authority comes from **within the POM function**. Due to the size of the task involved and its relative importance for a small business, getting this right and handling transition well will affect its likelihood of continuing success. To help in this difficult handover, the rest of this section outlines some useful procedures.

1. **Making knowledge available**. Any incumbent will enjoy the advantage of being the person most familiar with the ins and outs of the job: this is especially true in POM. Because of the amount of detail involved much of the essential knowledge is kept in the operations manager's head – there are usually no guidelines requiring it to be put on paper. This knowledge comes from a lifetime of being at the centre of decisions and being the person who has the final word. Again, this is especially true for companies at the lower end of the small business spectrum. An important step to improve the transition involved in management succession is thus **to make this information available**.

2. **Taking stock of the information**. One way of creating a source of reference for relevant information is committing it to paper. This provides a checklist for both the incumbent and the new manager. For the latter it will help reduce the number of false starts and help separate the key issues involved. This will make picking up the important aspects of the job easier.

The list will also generate a number of tasks and can form another area for discussion between the old and new management team. The chapter headings of this book would provide a good starting point when constructing such a list.

3. **Sharing the management**. The new manager should be designated (and brought in if he is from outside) quickly, in order to ensure that as much overlap as possible can be provided. Such a 'warm-up period' will help the transition. The key internal and external links can thus be forged in a thoughtful atmosphere and the

maximum advantages which can accrue from such planning will be obtained.

4. **Reviewing progress**. It is most important that, this transition having once been established, things are not left to drift. The new manager and the new business will gain much advantage from the **formal progress reviews** which need to be set up at the time of change and which record ongoing progress on a regular basis.

Conclusion

One area in which small businesses have a distinct advantage over medium-sized and large organisations is that of **people**. Having control over the business and involving a relatively small organisation, the opportunity to structure employment and remuneration policies is unique. The day-to-day pressures of markets and production/operations activities are real and compulsive. For this reason, issues such as payment, employee involvement and management succession often stay on the side lines, evolving without adequate or suitable direction. The opportunity to harness this considerable asset is, therefore, lost to the business. Its **intangible** nature leads to a situation where it is put aside whilst attention is directed to those factors which tangibly affect the 'bottom line.'

It was the failure of businesses to realise (and to work to obtain) these advantages which led to the comment by one worker that in a large company you are **just a number** whilst in a small company you are **just a name**.

Select Bibliography

Chapters 1 and 2

M. H. Abdelsamad and A. T. Kindling, 'Why small businesses fail', *Advanced Management Journal*, Spring 1978, pp. 24–32.

Background to the Government Small Firms Policy, Small Firms Division, Department of Trade and Industry, November 1983

Bolton Committee Report, *Report of the Committee of Inquiry on Small Firms*. (Chairman J. E. Bolton), Cmnd 4811, November 1971, HMSO.

British Graduate Association, *High Management Education and The Production Function*, November 1977.

W. Di Petro and B. Sawhney, 'Business failures, managerial competence and macreconomic variables', *American Journal of Small Business* 11(2), October 1977, pp. 4–15.

J. P. Edwards (Director, Centre for Enterprise Policy Studies, University of Bath), 'Social and political pressures upon the small firm: the role of the small business in a future society', EFMD Thirteenth Small Firms Conference, Vienna, September 1983.

R. W. T. Gill and K. G. Lockyer, *The Career Development of the Production Manager in British Industry*, BIM, 1979.

T. J. Hill, *Production/Operations Management* Prentice-Hall, 1983.

―――――, 'Production/Operations Management', Chapter 19 in K. Elliot and P. Lawrence, *Introducing Management*, Penguin Books, 1985a.

―――――, *Manufacturing Strategy – the Strategic Management of Manufacturing Function*, Macmillan, 1985b.

―――――, *et al.*, 'The Production Manager's Task and Contribution', Working Paper 94, IMRAD, University of Warwick, July 1981.

S. P. Hutton and P. A. Lawrence, *Production Managers in England and Germany*, report to the Department of Industry, 1978.

N. R. Land, 'Too much emphasis on management assistance?', *Journal of Small Business Management* 13(3), July 1975, pp. 1–5.

P. A. Lawrence, *Operations Management: Research and Priorities*, report to the Social Sciences Council, April 1983.

K. G. Lockyer and S. Jones, 'The Function Factor', *Management Today*, September 1980.

―――――― *et al.*, *Production Management within the United Kingdom*, University of Bradford Management Centre, 1980.

C. McKee, 'Why so many businesses fall by the way side', *Rydges* December 1978, pp. 58–9.

M. K. McQuillan, *Graduate Engineers in Production*, Cranfield Institute of Technology, 1978.

Robson Rhodes Report, Department of Trade and Industry, 1983, HMSO.

US Government Printing Office, *The state of small business: a report to the President*, March 1984.

Wilson Report, *Interim Report of the Committee to Review the Functioning of Financial Institutions – the financing of small firms*, Cmnd 7503, March 1979, HMSO.

Chapter 3

J. Dewhurst and P. Burns, *Small Business: Finance and Control*, Macmillan, 1983.

D. Donleavy, 'Causes of Bankruptcy in England', in A. Gill and T. Webb (eds), *Policy Issues in Small Business Research*, Saxon House, 1980.

R. H. Hayes and S. C. Wheelwright, 'Link manufacturing process and product life cycles', *Harvard Business Review*, January/February 1979, pp. 133–40.

W. Heilrich, 'The TOWS matrix – a tool for situational analysis', *Long Range Planning* 15(2), 1982, pp. 54–66.

T. J. Hill, *Production/Operations Management*, Prentice-Hall, 1983.

————, *Manufacturing Strategy – the Strategic Management of the Manufacturing Function*, Macmillan, 1985.

W. E. Sasser *et al.*, *Management of Service Operations*, Alyn & Bacon, 1978.

Chapter 4

Bolton Committee Report, *Report of the Committee of Inquiry on Small Firms* Cmnd 4811, November 1971, HMSO.

Business Monitor Report on the Census of Production Summary Tables, PA 1002, 1981, HMSO.

A. C. Cooper, 'R & D is more efficient in small companies', *Harvard Business Review*, May–June 1964, pp. 78–83.

J. H. Davison, 'Why most new consumer brands fail', *Harvard Business Review*, March/April 1976, pp. 117–22.

J. Dewhurst and P. Burns, *Small Business: Finance and Control*, Macmillan, 1983.

M. Gibbons and D. S. Watkins, 'Innovation and the small firm', *R & D Management* 1(1), October 1970, pp. 340–8.

T. J. Hill, *Manufacturing Strategy – the Strategic Management of the Manufacturing Function*, Macmillan, 1985.

K. R. Jeffrey *et al.*, 'Design in small manufacturing companies in Scotland', paper presented at the 6th Annual National Small Firms Policy and Research Conference, September 1983.

B. Johannisson and C. Lindstrom, 'Firm size and inventive activity', *Swedish Journal of Economics* 4, 1971, pp. 427–42.

J. Langrish *et al.*, *Wealth from Knowledge*, Macmillan, 1972.

J. F. Lowe and N. K. Crawford, 'Technology Licensing and the small and medium-sized firm', *European Small Business Journal* 1(4), 1982, pp. 11–24.

———, *Innovation and Technology Transfer in the Growing Firm*, Pergamon Press, 1984.

R. S. Mason, 'Product diversification and the small firm', *Business Policy* 3(3), 1973, pp. 28–39.

National Science Foundation, 'Indicators of International Trends in Technological Innovation', NSF C889, April 1976.

M. Oakley, 'Product design and development in small firms', *Design Studies* 3(1), January 1982, pp. 5–10.

OECD, 'Government policies and factors influencing the innovation capability of SMEs', paper prepared by the OECD Secretariat and Staff Groups Strategic Surveys, May 1978.

D. E. Robinson, 'Style changes: cynical, inexorable and forseeable', *Harvard Business Review*, November/December 1975, pp. 121–31.

R. Rothwell, 'The characteristics of successful innovators and technically progressive firms (with some comments on innovation research)', *R & D Management* 7(3), 1977, pp. 191–206.

———, 'Small and medium-sized manufacturing firms and technical innovations', *Management Decision* 16(6), 1978, pp. 349–59.

F. C. Schwarz, 'Value analysis for small business', *Journal of Small Business Management* 12(2), April 1974, pp. 34–40.

T. Webb *et al.* (eds), *Small Business Research*, Gower, 1982.

Chapter 5

A. J. Beaumont, 'Location, Mobility and Finance of High Technology Companies in the UK Electronics Industry', Department of Industry, South East Regional Office, November 1982, unpublished.

British Steel Corporation, *Starting from cold*, 1982; this gives details of the BSC workshop complexes established throughout Britain (at December 1981, the first 200 housed 160 businesses and 750 people).

Department of Industry, *Provision of Small Industrial Premises*, March 1980, HMSO.

———, 'Helping small Firms Start-up and Grow: Common Services and Technological Support', 1982, HMSO.

J. P. Edwards (Director, Centre for Enterprise Policy Studies, University of Bath), 'Social and political pressures upon the small firm: the role of small business in a future society', EFMD Thirteenth Small Firms Conference, Vienna, September 1983.

M. Gaffney, *Running your own Business – planning for success*, Department of Trade and Industry, 1984, HMSO.

F. F. Gilmore 'Formulating strategy in smaller companies', *Harvard Business Review*, May/June 1971, pp. 71–80.

H. H. Hand *et. al*, 'Economic feasibility analysis for retail location', *Journal of Small Business Management* 13(3), July 1979, pp. 28–35.

I. C. MacMillan, 'Strategy and flexibility in the smaller business', *Long Range Planning*, June 1975, pp. 62–3.

J. Noar, 'How to make strategic planning work for small businesses', *Advanced Management Journal*, Winter 1980, pp. 35–9.

Robson Rhodes Report, Department of Trade and Industry, 1983, HMSO.

R. N. Sexton and R. D. Dahle, 'Factors affecting long-range planning in the small business firm', *Marquette Business Review*, Winter 1976, pp. 158–65.

Small Business Administration, 'Business plan for small manufacturers', Management Aids 2.007, 1983, and 'Business plan for small service firms', Management Aids 2.022, 1983, are available free of charge from SBA, PO Box 15434, Forth Worth, Texas 76119, USA.

Derek Waterworth, *Marketing for the Small Business*, Macmillan, 1977.

J. G. Whacker and J. S. Cromatie, 'Adapting forecasting methods to the small firm', *Journal of Small Business Management* 17(3), *July 1979*, pp. 1–7.

S. C. Wheelright, 'Strategic planning in the small business', *Business Horizons*, August 1971, pp. 51–8.

Chapter 6

G. Friedrichs and A. Schaff (eds), 'Microelectronics and Society. For better or for worse', a Report to the Club of Rome, Pergamon Press, 1983, p. 53.

N. Gaither, *Production and Operations Management*, Dryden Press, 1980.

R. W. Hall and T. E. Vollman, 'Planning your material requirements', *Harvard Business Review*, September/October 1978, pp. 105–12.

A. Hulse, 'Micro-processors and the Small Business', Department of Industry, December 1980, pp. 7–8.

J. Martin, *Application Development Without Programmers*, Prentice-Hall, 1982.

S. Mendham, 'Modernisation of small businesses in the UK', paper presented at the 10th International Small Businesses Conference, Singapore, 12–15 September 1983.

J. Orlicky, *Materials Requirement Planning*, McGraw-Hill, 1975.

G. W. Plossl, *Manufacturing control – the last frontier for profits*, Reston Publishing Co., 1973.

J. W. Rice and T. Yosbikawa, 'A comparison of Kanban and MRP concepts for the control of repetitive manufacturing systems', *Production and Inventory Management* 73(1), 1982, pp. 1–14.

R. J. Schonberger, *Operations Management*, Business Publications, 1981.

W. J. Stevenson, *Production/Operations Management*, Irwin, 1982.

B. Taylor and K. Davis, 'Increasing productivity through work-in-progress management', *Production and Inventory Management* 18(1), 1978.

T. E. Vollman, W. L. Berry and D. C. Wybark, *Manufacturing Planning and Control Systems*, Irwin, 1984.

O. W. Wight, *Production and inventory management in the computer age*, CBI Publishing Co., 1974.

FURTHER INFORMATION ON COMPUTERS

1. Training materials are available, including general 'awareness' training videos, from Video Arts, 2nd Floor, Bunbarton House, 68 Oxford Street, London W1N 9LA (01–637 7288). They also provide booklets introducing computers at an elementary level. Most major suppliers provide their own training courses, manuals and materials for more specific purposes, but increasingly there is available a range of local courses from training specialists particularly for popular software like Wordstar, Lotus and Database II.

2. The National Computing Centre will provide advice on all aspects of computing, including, free of charge, easy to read information on choosing computers, software and support services. They have offices at:

Oxford Road
Manchester M1 7ED
061–228 6333

11 New Fetter Lane
London EC4A 1PU
01–353 4875

7th Floor, Devonshire House
Great Charles Street
Birmingham B3 2PL
021–236 6283

117 Lisburn Road
Belfast BT9 7BP
0232–665997

2nd Floor, Anderston House
389 Argyle Street
Glasgow G2 8LR
041–204 1101

6th Floor, Bristol & West Building
41 Corn Street
Bristol BS1 1HG
0272–277077

Chapter 7

J. L. Burbidge, *Production Planning*, Heinemann, 1971.

T. J. Hill, *Production/Operations Management*, Prentice-Hall, 1983.

T. J. Hill, *Manufacturing Strategy: The Strategic Management of the Manufacturing Function*, Macmillan, 1985.

H. F. Mather, 'Manufacturing control in perspective', *Production and Inventory Management* (4), 1976, pp. 36–45.

J. Orlicky, *Materials Requirement Planning*, McGraw-Hill, 1975.

G. W. Plossl, *Manufacturing Control – the last frontier for profits*, Reston Publishing Co., 1973.

Small Business Administration, 'Pointers on scheduling production', Management Aids 2.003, SBA, PO Box 15434, Fort Worth, Texas 76119, USA.

R. J. Schonberger, *Japanese Manufacturing Techniques: Nine Hidden Lessons in Simplicity*, Free Press, 1982.

D. F. Tooley, *Production Control Systems and Records*, Gower, 1985.

T. E. Vollman, W. L. Berry and D. C. Whybark, *Manufacturing Planning and Control Systems*, Irwin, 1984.

O. W. Wight, *Production and inventory control in the computer age*, CBI Publishing Co., 1974.

Chapter 8

I. Beronlak, 'To improve productivity in small business. Why? How?', paper presented at the 11th European Business Small Seminar on Productivity, Helsinki, 15–18 September 1981.

BIM, 'Added Value: An Introduction to Productivity Schemes', MSO 40 (M. Woodmansey), 1978.

R. Caplan, *A practical approach to quality control*, Business Books, 1971.

J. B. Coates, 'Productivity: what is it?', *Long Range Planning* 13, August 1980, pp. 90–7.

R. M. Currie, *Work Study*, 4th edn, Pitman, 1977.

G. E. Hayes and H. G. Laing, *Modern Quality Control*, Bensiger, Bruce and Glencoe, 1977.

T. J. Hill, *Production/Operations Management*, Prentice-Hall, 1983.

ILO, 'Introduction to Work Study', 2nd edn, 1969.

G. P. Latham and S. B. Kinne, 'Improving job performance through training in goal setting', *Journal of Applied Psychology* 59(2), 1974, pp. 187–91.

———— and L. M. Saari, 'The importance of union acceptance for productivity improvement through goal setting', *Personnel Psychology* 35, pp. 781–7.

Small Business Administration, 'Setting up a quality control system', Management Aids 2.012, SBA, PO Box 15434, Fort Worth, Texas 76119, USA.

Chapter 9

D. S. Ammer, 'Is your purchasing department a good buy', *Harvard Business Review*, March/April 1974, pp. 36–44; 54–9.

Business Monitor Report on the Census of Production Summary Tables, PA 1002, 1981, HMSO.

P. Baily and D. Farmer, *Managing Materials in Industry*, Gower, 1972.

————, *Purchasing Principles and Management*, 4th edn, Pitman, 1983.

T. J. Hill, *Production/Operations Management*, Prentice-Hall, 1983.

C. K. Lysons, *Purchasing*, Longman, 1981.

D. C. Moore and H. E. Fearon, 'Computer-aided decision-making in purchasing', *Journal of Purchasing*, November 1973, pp. 5–25.

W. J. Parsons, *Improving purchasing performance*, Gower, 1982.

D. T. Wilson and H. L. Mathews, 'Impact of management information systems upon purchasing decision-making', *Journal of Purchasing*, February 1971, pp. 48–56.

Chapter 10

L. B. Barnes and S. A. Hershon, 'Transferring power in the family business', *Harvard Business Review*, July/August, 1976, pp. 105–14.

J. Boswell, *The Rise and Decline of Small Firms*, Allen & Unwin, 1973.

R. Brown, 'When a business matures: how to keep the entrepreneurial thrust', *Management Review*, April 1980, pp. 14–17.

A. Dastmalchian and R. Mansfield, 'Payment systems in smaller companies: relationships with size and climate', *Personnel Review* 9(2), Spring 1980, pp. 27–32.

Department of Trade and Industry, *Employing people: guidance for those setting up a business for the first time*, 1983, HMSO.

S. Flykt, 'Payment systems in smaller enterprises in Sweden', *Management Decision* 18(6), 1980, pp. 318–26, based on a paper given at the 11th European Small Business Seminar, Helsinki, 15–18 September 1981.

T. J. Hill, *Production/Operations Management*, Prentice-Hall, 1983.

S. S. Liao, 'The effect of the size of firms on managerial attitudes', *California Management Review* XVIII (2), Winter 1975, pp. 59–65.

M. McCarthy, 'Should your firm consider the flexitime alternative', *Industrial Engineering*, January 1981, pp. 50–1; 55–9; 89.

C. McGivern, 'The dynamics of management succession', *Management Decision* 16(1), Spring 1978.

S. Matsumoto (Vice-President, Tokyo Small Investment Co. Ltd), 'Modern management: the road to prosperity for medium-sized business', paper given at the 10th International Small Businesses Conference, Singapore, 12–15 September 1983.

Merrett–Cyntiax Associates, 'The Dynamics of Small Firms', *Committee of Inquiry on Small Firms*, research report 12, 1971, HMSO.

T. I. Patterson, *Job Evaluation – A Practical Guide*, BIM, 1967.

————, Job Evaluation, *Business Books*, 1972.

A. E. B. Perrigo, 'Delegation and succession in the small firm', *Personnel Management*, May 1975, pp. 35–7.

E. F. Schumacher, *Small is Beautiful*, Blond Briggs, 1973.

P. C. Schumacher, unpublished papers, 1979–81, Schumacher Projects, Church House, Godstone, Surrey RH9 8BW.

E. G. Wood, *Bigger Profits for the Small Firm*, Business Books, 1978.

Index

216